Table of Contents

Table of Contents

Introduction

You've set your goals. You have your dreams. You know what you want and where you *hope* to be. The question is, how do you get there? How do you get from where you are right now to become the goal-smashing, successful, driven individual you want to be? *With better focus.*

Before you can learn to run, you must first learn how to crawl. Before you can begin successfully accomplishing one goal after another, you must first master the path paved towards that goal. That path is your ability to focus and concentrate. They say the path to success is filled with obstacles that will challenge you and push you beyond your comfort zone every step of the way. One of those challenges comes in the form of focus. Your ability to stay focused is going to be the defining factor that separates success from failure. You could have the motivation, the desire, the dream, and the willpower to achieve, but if you're not *focused* enough to stay on track, all of that is not going to help you anyway.

Imagine success is a road, and the car you're driving to get you to your ultimate destination is the focus. The car (focus) must stay on the designated path and not veer off course to arrive at the destination the way you intended. Keeping the "car" on track is not as easy as it sounds because of the distractions that we need to overcome each day. Emails, social media alerts, meetings, noisy environments, chatty colleagues, issues that keep coming up. With the intentional ability needed to stay focused, it becomes all too easy to succumb to these temptations, and before you know it, you've lost track and lost momentum.

Staying focused is an everyday problem, but it is not a problem you have to face alone. This guide is organized in the 7-step logical sequence of events needed that can help anyone, young or old, experienced or beginner, to learn the necessary steps they must take to improve their ability to focus. Follow this guide in the order it is presented and by the end of it, you'll have everything you need to shut down the distractions in your life and never struggle to try and maintain focus ever again.

There are plenty of guides on this subject on the market, thank you for choosing this one! Every effort was made to ensure it is full of as much useful information as possible. Please enjoy!

Chapter 1: The Focus Frame of Mind

Multitasking is a fallacy. There's a lot of truth in the old figure of speech that goes, *"A Jack of all trades is a master of none."* You simply cannot do your tasks *well* when your mind and your attention is scattered in all sorts of different directions. You may be able to do it, but perhaps not as *well* as you would have if you had been completely and utterly focused on a single task alone. Multitasking is the lie we have all been taught to believe that we could juggle several things at once and *still* achieve incredible success. Oh, it may work well in the beginning, and you feel like you're pulling off an impossible feat. Your colleagues watch with admiration, and you seem like an unstoppable force that just keeps going, going, going. But it won't be long before you end up burned out, stressed out, and depleted of any mental energy needed to focus on the remainder of the work that needs to get done.

No, the truth is, multitasking robs you of your focus. It stops you from achieving success and excelling at what you do. Imagine that you were running a race. In that race, there was only one goal, one outcome. Make it to the end and finish with a medal. As you stretch your muscles and line up at the starting block, that outcome becomes the only thing on your mind. As your legs pump and your heart pounds with each step you take, all you're focused on is crossing that finish line. You keep your eyes directly in front of you as you stride closer and closer. You don't look left, and you don't look right. Why? Because you know as soon as you do, you're in danger of being distracted by the other runners, possibly missing a step and tripping. Because you refuse to allow yourself that distraction by staying fixated on the finish line, you achieve the goal you set out to do. To cross that finish line and finish the race. That's what focus does.

It's been drilled into us from the time we were in school about how important focus was if we wanted to succeed. To stay mentally alert and focused at all times when you're undertaking an important task. Yet, we continue to allow yourselves to get distracted and sidetracked, losing focus, and missing out on important information. If we know focus matters when it comes to success, why do we still allow yourselves to lose it? The answer is simple. There are *too many* distractions that we're faced with today. The closest constant distraction you have is probably next to you right now. Your mobile phone.

There's a lot of pressure and distraction in our busy, hectic world that can make focus a difficult thing to master. But those who have mastered it have learned to reap its incredible rewards, which is what you're here to do.

Understanding Focus and Why It Matters

Focus, in a nutshell, is your ability to direct your attention towards one thing and one thing alone. Focus is defined as deliberate action. You're *deliberately* concentrating on the one thing that you need to, and you're intentional about it. Two types of focus come into play:

- **Automatic Focus** - This type of focus is generally short-lived, lasting perhaps 10-12 seconds. It keeps us alert to detect any possible dangers within our immediate environment. Like looking both ways before you cross the street, for example. Or when you hear an unexpected noise that startles you and gets your attention. Automatic focus distracts from what you were doing previously to momentarily direct your attention elsewhere.

- **Intentional Focus** - This, we consciously control. Intentional focus happens when we *want* or *need* to pay attention to something. When you've got a report for work to finish, you need to intentionally focus on your mind on that. To concentrate until you get it done. This type of focus usually needs discipline and willpower to sustain it for a prolonged period.

Neuroscientist Russell Poldrack's research highlights just how damaging the bottleneck effect of multitasking can be. Our memories, both long and short term, were not built to handle a lot of information at a single time. Information at best can be retained for about 10 seconds, and overloading the short-term memory interrupts the information flow we receive. For example, if you interrupted your reading of this chapter by stopping to respond to a text instead of responding *after* you're done, the information flow from your working memory to your long-term memory is disrupted. Long-term memory is where we store data and copious amounts of other information, ready for retrieval in the future when needed. When you're not concentrating on what you're reading, information is not transferred effectively to your short and long-term memory. You won't retain the information you read in this chapter, and you definitely won't be able to apply it later because you won't remember.

To focus, you must immerse yourself completely in the task you're undertaking. To cast aside all distractions for a certain time until you're done with what you need to do. We all have the ability within us to focus for an extended period when we should. The only obstacle in your path now is the discipline and willpower to do it. Getting into the focus frame of mind is easier when you enjoy what you do or if what you're engaged in is something you're passionate about. Only when you're tasked with something you don't enjoy does focus become a challenge. The ability to focus would vary from person to person. Some people are better at it than others, but the good news is, you can train yourself to achieve the level of focus you desire, and it begins by setting your goals.

Why Goals Are Important for Better Focus

Goals are the key to staying focused until the end, just like the example before about running a race. Without a goal, what would be your motivation for crossing the finish line? To block out any distractions that could put you in danger of losing the race? When a goal is aligned with a passion or desire, it becomes *even more* powerful than ever.

There's a lot that has been written about the importance of setting goals, and you probably already understand on some level why goals matter. Aside from motivating you to boost your productivity, goals matter in helping you remain focused because:

- **It Makes You Stronger in the Face of Challenges** - When you *know* what you want to achieve and why you need to do it, it makes you mentally more resilient against the challenges that come your way. Without a goal and a purpose, it would be all too easy to give in to the temptation of giving up.

- **It Helps You Make Better Decisions** - Goals give you a sense of direction, a path that paves the way about where you should go, and what you need to do to get there. If you were driving, your goal would be the map that gets you to the destination. When you know where you're going, you make better decisions along the way. Goals make you reflect on the actions you take. You ask yourself *"Is this going to lead me one step closer to my goal?"*. Your answer will determine the direction you go and every decision that is made should be a decision that leads you one step closer to your goal.

- **They Spur You to Action** - A goal compels you to keep moving forward. To get up and do something because you have a purpose. Let's say you intended to purchase a new car. With that in mind, you set a goal for yourself to save $1,000 by the end of 3-months. That specific goal then spurs the necessary action needed to accomplish that goal. You put aside more money for your savings, and you take on extra work you do overtime, whatever it takes to bring in that extra income that leads you closer to that goal.

- **It Helps You Sustain Momentum** - Seeing progress can be addictive. As you watch your car saving fund grow from $0 as it slowly inches its way to the $1,000 mark, the dopamine released in your brain triggers a snowball effect that keeps the momentum going. Once you've got into the groove and start seeing progress, you'll be addicted to keeping the ball rolling.

- **They Build Confidence** - Each time you see yourself inching closer to a goal you thought was impossible in the beginning, your confidence is increased bit by bit. With each challenge or obstacle you overcome, your belief in your ability to do this is renewed. There are very few people in this world who manage to accomplish everything that they set out to do. Knowing that you're one of those people who are close to achieving success can be an extremely empowering feeling.

- **They Make You Accountable** - Without a goal, there's no sense of urgency to achieve what you need to within a certain timeframe. It can be a humbling and eye-opening experience when you look back at the goals you set for yourself in the past but didn't quite accomplish. When you realize that you could have done it if only you had been more committed, the new goals you set for yourself will strengthen your resolve as you take on that responsibility knowing that success is entirely in your hands right now. You and you alone can turn your dream into a reality, but it is up to you to do something about it.

Staying focused can be hard, but not impossible. Motivation will fizzle and fluctuate with time and stress, which is why it is important to have goals to remind you to keep going in the moments you wonder why you're doing this. Goals are great, but it is important not to have too many at a time since it defeats the purpose of focus. Ideally, you should have no more than 1-3 goals at any given time, and if there is more than one, that goal should be linked to the first one. Even daily, you should have no more than three primary tasks or goals per day that become your main focus and priority.

Chapter 2: Step 1 – Building Your Environment

The first step of the 7-step program to focus your mind is to start with building the right environment that is going to facilitate your focus. Most people these days struggle to stay focus because of the shorter attention spans we have. The digital age we live in has a role to play on that front. A study by the Technical University of Denmark confirmed that today, we are being faced with more information than we were several years ago, and while we have more things to focus on, our *ability* to focus is diminishing. According to the study, the reason behind this shorter attention span is the urge for constant "newness" that has emerged because of the increasing volume of content. When we keep looking for what the next "new" thing us, we switch topics more frequently.

Microsoft had an even more interesting take on the subject. In a 2015 study, Microsoft claimed that the average person has an eight-second attention span, which they claimed was less than the attention span of a goldfish. That number, by the looks of it, is shrinking every year with our increasing dependence on our digital connectivity. Microsoft Canada's consumer insights lead, Alyson Gausby, said no matter what environment we find ourselves in, our survival depends on our ability to remain focused.

The Right Environment Matters More Than Motivation

You could have your goals set and motivation by the bucket load, but if your environment is not designed to facilitate focus, you're going to struggle to stay on track. You've got your computer ready at the desk prepared to work but end up getting distracted by social media, standing up frequently to stretch or walk around, making yourself a cup of coffee, going to the bathroom, chatting with friends. Anything *except* sitting down for a sustained period focusing on your task. You know you've got a deadline, but you "can't help" getting distracted. Or can you?

If you've fallen behind on your task or goals one too many times, it's time to say enough is enough. Something needs to change, and that something starts with your environment. If you're tired of always having to rush to meet deadlines, scramble to get things done at the last minute, sacrificing a few nights of sleep to burn the midnight oil as you work through the night trying to get things done, your environment needs to change and fast.

Most people believe the ability to focus on a task comes down to self-discipline and the willpower not to move from your desk until you've done what you need to do. Unfortunately, that's a misguided belief. It has never been more imperative that we eliminate distractions that rob us of precious time. Specifically, we can be more aware of the time we are wasting on social media or web-browsing.

Building the Right Kind of Environment

As a modern society, we have been told that multitasking is helpful to get things done. Your internet browser probably has multiple tabs open at any given time, and your phone is most likely beside you and interrupting at intervals even as you read this. This has become the norm; it is how we live. But have you ever tried to text and drive at the same time? There is a reason it is dangerous. Doing multiple things at once means that nothing gets done well or efficiently. You *know* you want to improve your focus and concentration. You've probably thought about it several times even before you started reading this. In truth, the answer to getting started was right in front of you all along. *Change your environment.*

It's incredible what little tweaks in the environment can do. To better maintain focus, you need to now design and set up an environment for yourself that is free from any kind of distraction. Both digitally and physically. Take a long, hard look at your current surroundings. Is your environment helping you boost your productivity or serving as a distraction because it keeps moving your focus away from what you're supposed to be doing? It is time for an assessment of your current environment to see what elements need to be changed and removed.

- **Adjust Your Environment to Suit You** - It's a mobile world we live in these days. With more opportunities to work remotely and on the go, there may be times when we find ourselves having to work at different locations. When that happens, setting up your perfect space can be a challenge, but it's still doable. Depending on where you are, make little tweaks and adjustments to your space until you feel comfortably satisfied with the outcome. If you have to share a desk at work, put a plant between you and your chatty colleague to minimize distraction. Angle your computer away from any distractions. Clear the table of any clutter and put it aside temporarily. Put on noise-canceling headphones for better concentration.

- **Getting Rid of Clutter** - There's a reason why minimalists keep their desk practically empty with nothing on it except a laptop, and maybe one pen and notepad for urgent notes. Clutter is a distraction, and building an environment that facilitates focus means you're going to need to declutter your desk fast. Get rid of the unnecessary pens, paper, mugs, random bits, and pieces of miscellaneous items, anything that is *not* contributing to your task should not be on your desk. Go minimalist and declutter your workspace and see what a difference it makes when there's nothing except you and your laptop alone.

- **Ergonomic Comfort** - Aside from being better for your overall health and to minimize injury, ergonomic workspaces improve your productivity. It's easy to stay focused when you're comfortable and not fidgeting left and right, trying to get into a comfortable position. Ergonomic workspaces are more than just making sure you're in a well-lit environment or that your chair is comfortable enough. It involves the way your worktop is positioned and that it is adjusted to a height that promotes good posture for you. Your desk should be at a height that is comfortable enough for you to type and work for a long time if needed, and your chair should be designed to support good posture to avoid any muscle tension or aches and pains from sitting down too long.

- **A Well-Lit Environment** - It can be hard to concentrate when you're squinting and trying to get as close to your screen as possible to make out the words. Having to re-read sentences multiple times is not conducive to productivity, and the frustration of not being able to see is going to disrupt your ability to focus. Natural lighting is the best, although not always possible. If that's the case, opt for ambient lighting to avoid the glare bouncing off your computer screens. When reading documents or books, an adjustable, low-glare lamp works best, so your reading material is always well-lit.

- **Disconnect from Social Media** - Or any digital device that is not going to actively contribute to your task. The internet is addictive and as helpful as it has no doubt been, it is also a major cause of distraction. It's hard to knuckle down and try to get any work done when your phone is beeping every couple of minutes with one notification after another. Disconnect from social media, turn off your phone, tuck it away in your desk and make it a rule not to pick up any digital device or browse any pages on the internet that are not related to your task.

- **One Window at A Time Rule** - Tying in with the point before about disconnecting from social media is to make it a rule to only have one window on your computer open at a time. You don't need multiple tabs because those are nothing more than distractions. It may seem like no big deal, but your subconscious is bothered by the unnecessarily overwhelming number of tabs you've got open. Focus requires only *one thing* at a time; that's a rule of thumb. Make it a rule to have only *one* tab open at any given time when you need to focus.

- **The Quiet Zone** - This may be hard to accomplish when you're stuck in a busy office, but where possible, ensure the environment you're working in is quiet and free from noisy distractions. It's easier to set up such a space in your home, although you might need to test out a few different locations before you find "the one." Some people work best in the quiet tranquility of the library. Others find their calming zone at the local coffee shop with their headphones on. Seek out empty meeting rooms in your office where you can sit for a few hours quietly focused on your work if you find your cubicle far too distracting. Change your location, change your environment, and find one that you're most comfortable in.

- **The Right Temperature** - Staying focused when you're just getting started is easy. After a while, though, being too hot or too cold is going to start to get to you. It won't be long before your discomfort is going to distract you from your task, so adjust the temperature to a comfortable level before you sit down and begin your task. If you're in an environment where you don't have full control over the temperature, like when you're working in your office or a public space, for example, come prepared with enough water and proper clothing to either stay hydrated or stay warm, depending on what you need.

- **Get Some Plants -** Interestingly enough, <u>NASA</u> has proven that some houseplants that can improve the quality of the air indoors. Having natural, green plants in your workspace creates a more serene ambiance, and better air quality leads to better focus when you've got a good amount of healthy oxygen flowing to your brain.

As admirable as our determination to stay focused is, there's only so much we can do before we eventually feel tired and need a break. Rather than forcing yourself to keep doing when you feel your focus waning, scheduling planned breaks can actually lead to better focus. At least, that's what a <u>study</u> by the University of Illinois claimed. In their research, they discovered that when the participants of the study who were tasked with working for 50-minutes were given short breaks in between, their performance was much better than those who tried to work straight through without any breaks at all. Based on the study's findings, this phenomenon was referred to as "vigilance decrement." In other words, losing focus over a period. Shorter breaks were a way to re-energize and recharge your brain, so it comes back to the task fresh and with renewed focus.

Chapter 3: Step 2 – Brainpower

Part of working to improve your focus is about building mental toughness and brainpower you need as you prove to yourself that you can handle anything. Staying on track and focused on your task is not always an easy thing to do. Even harder when you're surrounded by distraction. The ability to concentrate has become a skill, and luckily, it is a skill that can be developed by first working to enhance your mental prowess.

Before you begin, do a quick assessment of where the strength of your mental focus currently is. Your focus is looking good if you find it easy to remain alert when you need to, set goals, and accomplish them, feel recharged after taking short breaks and come back to your task with renewed motivation and a good amount of focus. Your mental focus might need some work done if you can't seem to block out distractions, struggle to concentrate, find your thoughts drifting aimless or daydreaming frequently, and if you find it hard to track your progress. Understanding where you stand right now will make the next few steps easier.

Our brains are just like every other muscle in your body. If we don't use it, eventually it will start to deteriorate. Your brainpower is crucial to your ability to focus. If you don't learn how to control your mind and become the master of your thoughts, then your mind will inevitably end up *controlling you.* That's when distractions and daydreams easily take over.

Willpower and Brainpower

The prefrontal cortex of the human brain controls our decision-making, our ability to plan for the future, and make choices that benefit us in the long run. The choice to focus so you can excel in whatever it is you take responsibility for. The prefrontal cortex is in the front of the skull behind the eyes, and studies have mapped what the brains of those with weak and strong will power look like. Differences in activity were detected in this area of the brain. But what does willpower have to do with brainpower? Sometimes distracting thoughts can be so overwhelming that we give in to temptation and find ourselves getting, well, distracted. Fighting off the temptation to remain focus is going to require a lot of willpower on your part because you need to now train yourself to deliberately ignore these distractions to keep yourself focused on what you're doing right this minute. When the motivation to stay focused fails, the next logical step is to turn to willpower.

Willpower is a limited resource, and it takes a great deal of energy to go against our natural inclinations and exercise the power of our will. The next time you're in the middle of typing out an urgent report and your phone beeps with a text you've been waiting for, observe how hard it is to fight your natural inclination to pick up that phone and immediately respond to the next. Ignoring it and staying focused on the report you're meant to be writing takes a lot of hard work and willpower, and when you're working that hard to concentrate, your brain is too. Sometimes, despite your best efforts, your brain needs a little help to keep going, and that help comes in the form of willpower until you've trained your brain to be strong enough to the point it no longer gets distracted or give in to the temptation of distraction as easily as it once did.

Brainpower Can Be Developed

How do professional athletes seem to maintain the optimal performance that they need at every game? Because they know how important it is to focus on the present game. They know how important it is to block out the distractions that threaten to take away their concentration, whether those distractions are internally or externally caused. Even if they were to have a slip and lose concentration for a moment, they can quickly gain it back again and return into the "zone." They manage to accomplish all of this and more by training and rewiring their brains. The ability for these athletes to stay alert and focused during their game is the difference between performances that is simply "alright," and performances that were "outstanding."

If outstanding is where you want to be, then it's time to start concentrating on the right things if you hope to improve and perform to your true potential. Like these professional athletes, we all have the power within us to be great at what we do. We just need to tap into it and hold onto those powers of concentration, especially when under intense pressure, as many athletes often find themselves going through.

What you're concentrating on matters just as much as *maintaining* your concentration. An example of focusing on the wrong thing would be when you're distracted thinking about what your colleague is doing and if they're going it better than you are instead of concentrating on the things *you should be doing* to excel. Another rule of thumb to keep in mind is that anything that does not actively contribute to your task is going to be a distraction. When you've got something you need to pay attention to, that should be the only thing that matters until you finish what you started.

Brainpower and the ability to concentrate can be trained with the right mental exercises. Like a muscle, your ability to focus needs to be strengthened with exercises. Eventually, it starts to get stronger over time, and your ability to concentrate for longer increases along with it. Train your brain and build its focus muscle with the following mental exercises:

- **An Object of Focus** - Find a quiet zone and place an object in front of you. This can be any object you like. It doesn't matter. Or if there's already an object in the room which you can comfortably look at in a seated position, go ahead with that.

- **Incremental Focus** - With the object ready, start focusing on it for a sustained period. Start with smaller time intervals, ranging between 3 to 5-minutes. Maintain your focus throughout that period, concentrating on nothing except the object in front of you. Once you're able to maintain this prolonged period of concentration without breaking it or getting distracted, slowly build on the time increments, increasing it gradually in stages. Bring it up to 10-minutes, then 15-minutes and so on. Train yourself over time to increase your concentration for longer and longer periods.

- **Memory Games** - Memory games are an excellent way to help you exercise your mental muscles and train your brain to enhance its powers of concentration over time. These games call for intense concentration if you want to win the game. Plus, it is a fun way to get in some mental training because these interactive games can easily be played anywhere on the go, and they're usually fun and interactive. If memory games are not your thing, there are other memory techniques that you could employ. Having to memorize stuff also forces you to concentrate on what you're doing to be successful at committing it to memory. If you prefer to read, train yourself to memorize at least one inspirational passage, quote, or saying each week as part of your memory strengthening exercises. Or perhaps even a passage out of your favorite book, maybe even a poem or two.

The Mindset of a Focused Winner

To develop the kind of focus that is the envy of others requires a certain level of mental toughness. The strongest and most successful people in the world are the ones who remain mentally tough and resilient in the face of obstacles that would have defeated others. Willpower, the drive, the determination, and the motivation to keep pushing forward, to keep challenging yourself to push beyond your boundaries are examples of the mental skills needed to stay focused and stay on track. To develop the mindset of a focused winner.

Prep yourself and your mind for anything that may come is the best way to build the brainpower of a mentally tough, resilient individual, and that can be accomplished by:

- **Always Be Ready for Change** - Our minds can be resistant to change when it's taking us out of our comfort zone. Life is not always going to go according to plan, and the more willing and prepared you are to adapt and change to the circumstances, the easier it will be for your brain to switch back into the focus mode it needs.

- **Detaching Yourself from Failures** - If you let it, your brain is going to hold onto the setbacks and failures of the past and keep you trapped in that endless cycle of mental negativity. This kind of thinking is a distraction, and it will take away your ability to stay focused on your goals unless you learn to detach yourself from your past failures. Setbacks happen to everyone, but what matters right now is how you recover and bounce back from it. Do you learn from the mistakes of the past? Or do you allow those mistakes to continually haunt your mind and stop you from moving forward?

- **Find Strength During Stress** - In times of great stress, hold onto the fact that stressful times are not going to last forever. Don't let your mind get too hung up over whatever stressful situation is happening to you right now. Thinking about it and replaying repeatedly in your mind how stressed you feel is only going to make you feel worse and do nothing for your concentration. In times of stress, find strength in the fact that this storm will eventually pass. You just need to be strong enough to get through it.

- **Be Patient** - Impatience is your brain's worst enemy. When you start focusing on how things are not moving as fast as you would like them too, that's all you're going to be able to think about. The more you obsess about it, the more precious time you lose. Time you could have spent doing something productive, leading you one step closer to your goal. Any goal that is worth achieving is not going to happen quickly, most of the time.

- **Don't Let Giving Up Be an Option** - *I am NOT a quitter. I will NOT give up.* Whenever you're tempted to quit, remind yourself that it is not an option. If the option to give up is always somewhere in your mind, the temptation will always be there. Once you start something, make it a commitment to yourself that you're not going to stop until you see it all the way to the end.

Chapter 4: Step 3 – Energy Management

Time may be your most precious resource, but it is not the only resource that matters. Yes, time is precious, and once a moment has passed, you'll never get it back again, but the thing about time is that it is still a *renewable* resource. An opportunity may have passed you by today, but there's always tomorrow to try again. Energy, however, is an entirely different matter. Once you're sick, tired, mentally drained, fatigued, or depleted of energy, even if you had one, two, or several hours on your hands, you're not likely to get anything productive done in that state. Focus is not even a possibility when your energy levels are running low, and this time, it is *energy management*, not time, that is what matters when it comes to improving your focus. Even with all the time in the world and motivation by the bucket load, it is unlikely you're going to accomplish much when you've got no energy to back up that motivation.

Today, it is not uncommon for many to spend long hours at the office. Again, that's fine because you've got time to do it, but your energy is another matter. Working longer hours doesn't guarantee a job well done when you don't have the energy and mental strength to focus on what you need to do. Still, the quest for better productivity and maximum efficiency continues, as many continue to find ways of optimizing the hours, they have a day to get more things done. Hence, multitasking, which we've established, may seem like it works well in the beginning, but it's not as effective as you may think. The answer to getting more done in a day is *not* multitasking. It's *energy management.*

Understanding Energy

Energy is the force that is responsible for giving the physical and mental strength needed to do the activities we're supposed to do. Energy is physical *and* mental. Physically, we get our energy from the food we consume and when we hydrate with water. Energy is renewed physically after a good rest or sleep session. As much as it may do for us, physical energy alone is not enough to get us to maintain the laser-sharp focus we need. It must work together with mental energy for optimal results.

The source of mental energy comes from a clear mind and healthy emotional management. Emotions that are left unregulated can wreak havoc on our mental capabilities. The next time you experience a highly emotional moment, observe the way you feel after the moment has passed. Do you suddenly find yourself feeling drained and faced with an overwhelming sense of tiredness? That all you want to do is lie down and sleep for several hours, hoping you'll feel better? Emotions are a powerful force, and when left uncontrolled, can cause immense mental fatigue that makes it difficult to get anything done, let alone concentrate.

Why Time Management Does Not Work

Time management is simply a way of describing how a person organizes and plans their time according to the specific activities and tasks that they need to do. At work, for example, you get eight hours to accomplish everything that you need to get, and it is up to you to divide your time and allocate how much time you are planning to spend on each activity. While this is great at helping you stay organized and stay on top of everything you need to do, it does very little in the way of helping you stay focused.

Looking busy should not be the primary goal. When someone is rushing around the office in a frenzy, or furiously clacking away at their keyboard with fervor, it doesn't necessarily mean they're handling their task as effectively as they should be. If you've ever found yourself in a situation where you felt like you were rushing about all day, yet felt at the end of the day that you hardly accomplished anything at all, this is why. It's because you're not *focused enough* to effectively to achieve results.

Time management systems simply do not work because that's not how *we were built to work*. Time management is great for us, but not for us because it doesn't take our energy levels into account. This system doesn't account for what happens when your willpower fluctuates or when your discipline might wan over the course of the day. Instead of scheduling your day around the tasks that must be done, what you should be doing is scheduling it *around your energy levels*. Let your energy be the deciding factor over which tasks should take priority.

If you continue to pursue the path of better time management, you're never going to improve your focus. Time management is ineffective in the long-run, and rather than promote better concentration, it promotes anxiety instead.

When you're chasing the clock instead of focusing on what you're supposed to be doing, you get nervous, flustered, and anxious when you notice you're running out of time. In the haste to meet the self-imposed time deadline you've set for yourself, your focus dissipates. Mistakes get made, crucial information gets overlooked, and you're feeling emotional from the pressure of rushing to meet your time goal so you can move onto your next task. Anxiety leads to stress, and stress leads to panic attacks and nervous meltdowns. In the end, nothing gets done anyway because of all these unforeseen interruptions that are a byproduct of time management. That is why, in the long run, time management is not an effective long-term strategy for focus and success. It's right up the same alley as multi-tasking. A fallacy and we need to stop entertaining these myths and misconceptions any longer for the sake of improving our ability to focus.

Strategies to Better Energy Management

Better energy management is possible when you've got the right strategies up your sleeve. Here's how you can get a better handle on yours, so you're not losing focus while trying to get more done:

- **Pace Yourself -** Feeling discouraged or overwhelmed just looking at your to-do list *before* you get started is sapping your mental energy. There may be a lot to do, but the key to doing it all is to pace yourself right from the start. Long-distance runners don't exhaust all their energy supply as soon as they leave the starting line. They start at a steady pace and maintain that momentum, so it's enough to sustain themselves until they reach the finish line. Avoid exhausting all your energy right from the start, pace yourself, listen to your body and take breaks when you need to recharge.

- **Optimize High-Energy Moments -** At certain points during the day, we experience spikes in our energy levels. This is when we feel fired-up and full of energy and ready to take on anything that comes our way. Energy levels fluctuate during the day, and you need to monitor the way you feel throughout the day and observe when those high-energy moments are. Use this time to tackle important tasks that require a greater level of focus and save the easier to handle tasks for when you need to take it slow to conserve energy.

- **Continuously Recharging** - Unlike robots, we were not built to work continuously for hours on end with the same level of energy or focus. Breaks are a necessity, and instead of seeing them as "time-wasters," start to see them for the opportunity that they are. An opportunity to recharge your mind and your body. The "powering through" mentality is nothing more than a myth. Powering through does not guarantee a job well done. Focus does. Listen to your body and when you feel yourself struggling to maintain focus, take a break.

- **Knowing Your Needs** - What do you need to feel recharged? What does it take for you to feel energized? Are you the extrovert who feels alive again after spending some time with people? Does a quick burst of exercise help you feel better? Maybe even sitting by the window enjoying the sunshine with a nice, warm cup of tea or coffee does the trick. Know what it takes for you to feel refueled and incorporate that into your daily routine. Whenever your energy levels are running low, pick it back up again by tapping into what makes you feel better.

- **Declutter Your Life** - Work is not the only culprit that tends to drain your energy; people do it too. You simply don't have enough time or energy on your hand to juggle *both* people that drain your energy and the unnecessary work in your day that take up more energy than it should. Energy management is going to call for decluttering. Declutter everything from your daily task list that is *not* a priority, and declutter the negative people in your life who do nothing more than make you feel exhausted each time you're in their company. Make it a point every three months or so to reassess your life and see if there's an improvement in your energy management after each decluttering session. If there's not much of an improvement, then maybe there's more decluttering that needs to get done.

- **Learning to Delegate** - There's only so much you can get done in a day. Instead of pushing yourself beyond and physical and mental limits, the better approach to take to help manage your energy levels is to learn how to delegate. If you know there is someone better suited to the task that could do a better job, don't be afraid to pass it along. That leaves you with more time, energy, and, better yet, *focus* to concentrate on what you should be doing. When you're in a leadership position, for example, part of being an effective manager is knowing the strengths and weaknesses of your team members and what each person brings to the table. This will help you to better delegate which person is equipped to handle the different tasks that your team will be presented with. A good leader is one that delegates the right jobs to the right people, so they come away with excellent results because they know just what to do when a job is given to them. Better yet, assigning a balanced workload to all team members equally makes it easier for everyone to focus on the single task that they are doing. Including you.

Chapter 5: Step 4 – Eliminating Procrastination

The reason we're sometimes guilty of procrastinating more than we should is
a lack of self-discipline. Well, that and laziness. When those two are
combined, they result in a deadly recipe for unproductivity. Self-discipline is
the one thing that separates an averagely talented person doing something
extraordinary and a naturally talented person doing something mediocre with
their lives, not using their talents to the fullest potential. Self-discipline is
something we can't see or touch or taste or smell, but its effects are
momentous.

Success in any aspect of life never happens in a total vacuum. An
individuals' determination, will power, intelligence, and a little bit of luck
determine the outcome of success. Apart from variables that you can control,
there is also the surrounding environment that you are in and the outside
circumstances that often influence success rates. To success, you must have a
burning desire and a reason to achieve it. The path to achieving goals is filled
with boredom, procrastination, anxiety, excuses, and difficulty. There will be
so many times that you will try to talk yourself out of this goal. But to keep
going, always remember the reason and the desire of why you wanted to
attain this goal because this helps you stay on track.

Procrastination Is Your Own Worst Enemy

procrastination – the mother of self-discipline problems. Most of us think 'I'll
do it later' when it comes to accomplishing our tasks that we've set out to do.
It is either you'll do it later, or you are waiting for the perfect time. For
example, our goal is to save money but then say, 'I'll wait till the first day of
the month to start.' Or if we are planning to exercise, we might say, 'I have to
get the right shoes.' Delaying and procrastinating is a hindrance that stops
you from achieving your goals. The more you delay, the more excuses you
come up with. The solution here is simple- is the delay you've given yourself
working for you? When you procrastinate, ask yourself- why are you doing
this? Is this benefitting you? If you delay things now- how will it impact you
in say, the next few hours? Will you need to leave work late? Do you have a
deadline catching up soon? Will this give you pressure? Questioning yourself
and making you accountable for your actions will help you overcome
procrastination or delaying things. Once you begin practicing this in your

self-discipline journey, you will enjoy doing things on time rather than delaying it.

Procrastination is one path that leads directly to laziness. When something can be done at that moment, but you choose to postpone it because you don't feel like doing it, which is indirectly indulging in laziness. Take, for example, a simple task such as washing the dishes. You know it needs to be done, it is easy enough to do right now, won't take up too much time, but how many times have you thought to yourself "I'll do it later." Then that later becomes another day, and another day and another day, and before you know it, you're looking at a mountain of dishes in the sink, which is now going to take you twice as long to get through. That's procrastination for you.

Then there's technology. Not just a distraction culprit, but a procrastination enabler too. It is unlike you're going to make it through an entire day without your phone lighting up, buzzing and vibrating several times without multiple texts, notifications, and alerts. It is just as unlikely that you're going to be able to make it through the entire day without checking your phone several times. Even as you sit behind your desk, typing out that urgent report for work, you *know* it's urgent, and you *know* the deadline is looming. Yet, you can't help it when your phone is right there next to you. The strong, inexplicable urge to pick it up is going to get to you eventually. Procrastination. It just kills your focus.

Presumably, the reason behind why we procrastinate is going to differ for each person. You procrastinate when your heart is not in it. You procrastinate when you're tired. You procrastinate when something more interesting comes along, and you'd rather be focused on that. Procrastination and a lack of focus are linked inexorably. When you're bored and unable to continue with the task you're supposed to be doing, it is likely the source of that boredom can be traced back to your dwindling ability to focus. As you lose interest, you become bored. Having distractions around you only exacerbates the issue.

Overcoming Procrastination Once and For All

Strategies are the best weapon that you have against your battle to overcome procrastination. Strategies give you a purpose and a clear direction to stay on track, it helps you set your priorities straight, and it can help simplify a lot of things which may otherwise feel like it is too much to handle.

- **Remove the Source of Temptation** - Before you settle into your work, look around you, and make a note of what the distractions are. Be honest about your assessment, because the only way to stay focused and not procrastinate is to remove all sources of temptation. If the temptation isn't there, you're less likely to give into it. If your *environment* is the cause of your distraction, find somewhere else to work. Whatever the source is, you must remove it to stay focused. Hold yourself accountable and make it your responsibility to ensure there's nothing around to tempt your focus away from your work.

- **Don't Try to Be Perfect** - Striving for "perfectionism" is going to put unnecessary pressure on you. When you're pressured, you're stressed. When you're stressed, you don't feel like doing work anymore. When you don't feel like it, you start sliding down that slippery procrastination slope until hours have passed and you're completely behind on your work. Aim to focus, so you know you're giving it the very best of your ability, and until you're satisfied you've done a good job. If you *can* make it perfect go ahead, but otherwise avoid putting that unnecessary pressure on yourself.

- **Get the Hard Tasks Over With** - The hardest tasks are the ones we always feel like procrastinating on the most. At the start of the day is when we have the most energy and fuel, so start your day with the hardest jobs first. If you've found yourself prone to procrastinating the harder tasks in the past and leaving them to the very last minute, try switching things around and start with the hard stuff first. When you're done with that hard task, move on to smaller, more doable tasks until the end of your workday. The next morning, repeat the process by selecting another hard task and starting your day off with that again. When you get the hard stuff out of the way, you find you feel much happier, lighter, and things seem more manageable somehow for the rest of the day.

- **Don't Be Too Hard on Yourself** - Procrastinators are their own worst enemy. You know procrastination is not good, yet you do it anyway and then feel bad about it and start criticizing yourself negatively for not having enough discipline and willpower to get the job done. Being too harsh on yourself is not going to resolve anything either, nor is it going to make it any easier for you to focus. Being stressed, worried that you're not good enough, feeling like a failure is only negative emotions that will drain you and make it harder for you to concentrate. When you know you procrastinated where you shouldn't have, acknowledge the mistake that you made and then commit to yourself to be more focused and disciplined moving forward.

Strategies to Improve Self-Discipline

Strategies for getting rid of bad procrastination habits on their own might not be as effective if a lack of self-discipline is still a problem. Therefore, you need to combine those tips *with* several strategies on hand that will help you build better self-discipline habits:

- **Set A Morning Routine at Work** - Commit to sticking to a morning work routine to get you into a more disciplined approach to managing your day. If you spend too much time procrastinating upon your arrival at work, a routine can help you fix that problem. Think about the things that you want to do the first thing you get into your office. Here's an example of how your morning routine at work can be. Switch on your computer. Make a cup of coffee. Read the newspaper. Speak to your co-workers who can catch up on work-related business. Check your calendar to see what you have scheduled for the whole week. Do tasks that require your immediate attention. Reply to emails. Start work.

- **Organizing Your Cubicle** - Or room, if you have one at the office. Organizing your workspace benefits all aspects of your life. An organized workspace makes you look forward to work every morning. It keeps your mind uncluttered, and it also helps with finishing tasks easily. Take some time off after your usual working hours to de-clutter your workspace. File papers, arrange books, organize your desk and drawers, and, most importantly- set this space up, so it is conducive and encouraging. Paste a large calendar on your office wall so you can see what's ahead of you. Put up some encouraging words, quotes, and even images. Place a mini terrarium on your desk to brighten up that space.

- **Practice Responsibility and Accountability** - By practicing self-discipline, we also learn to take more self-responsibility for our actions and thoughts. This is part of becoming self-disciplined adults. People who constantly complain and make excuses without taking responsibility are generally very unreliable and cannot be trusted. The first action to take today is to realize that this is your life. You are the hero to your own story, so each and every action you take will influence your storyline. From today onwards, resolve to take 100% responsibility for everything you are right now, and everything that you will become. Don't give excuses, don't complain, and don't explain.

- **Control Your Emotions** - People with self-discipline rarely let their emotions control their decisions. To become a responsible person, you need to take control of your emotions. You need to control your emotions, especially the negative ones, or they will control you. For today's action- practice forgiveness. Learn to accept that you have made a mistake and seek forgiveness. If someone has wronged you and apologized- accept the apology and move on.

- **Overcome Your Fear** - The biggest enemy of self-discipline is fear. Fear keeps you from taking the necessary actions because you rather stay in your comfort zone. You have to face fear if you want to make a change. Always tell yourself that you can do it because what doesn't kill you only makes you stronger. A disciplined person conquers fear, while a coward is controlled by fear. For today's action, identify your 3 biggest fears in life. Ask yourself- if you had just a day left to live, what would you do differently? Or what would you do differently if you know you couldn't fail.

Chapter 6: Step 5 – Shutting Down Distractions

Nobody likes being interrupted when they're trying to focus. That happens all too often, especially today, when mobile phones have dominated our everyday existence. To effectively focus, you are going to need to try to put away all the distractions before you settle down and start to work. Nearly everything you're surrounded with these days can be considered a form of distraction. Social media. Emails. Digital devices. Even people around you are a constant cause of distraction. For some, it is very easy to get sucked out of their focus zone at even the slightest disturbance. These distractions are not uncommon and the cost of being easily distracted, especially professionally, is well documented too.

University of California researchers discovered that when an office worker is interrupted, it typically takes 25-minutes before they can get back to their original task after the interruption. By then, the accuracy of their work has already decreased by 20%. So yes, being distracted when you're trying to focus your mind is something that needs to be addressed before it affects your productivity levels any longer.

We know distractions are bad for us, yet we do it anyway. Just like procrastination. No good can come of it, but somehow, we can't seem to stop ourselves from continually committing these bad habits. Avoiding distractions is hard. The temptation to give in has an immense pull, and it's not easy training your mind to stay on task for a sustained period. What makes it even harder is we were never *taught* the proper methods to maintain focus. When it comes to focusing your mind, most of us are left to our own devices to try and figure it out on our own. Add distractions into the mix, and it is no wonder we struggle to stay on track.

Overthinking Is A Form of Distraction

Another bad habit many of us engage in is overthinking. We overthink a lot of things in our lives, especially when we want something to go our way. But overthinking is another form of distraction, and the only way to do something about this is to rewire your brain to stop engaging in this habit. For chronic worriers, overthinking can cause negative consequences. It can also prevent us from enjoying the moment and, instead, keep us fixated on future uncertainties that make us anxious and worried when we lack control. Overthinking stops you from getting things done because you're too hung up on what could go wrong or what you're not doing enough of. Overthinking stops you from coming up with solutions to the problem because you're far too obsessed *about* the problem. Overthinking, of course, stops you from staying focused because there's simply too much going on in that busy mind of yours that it can't handle anything more.

Before we get into shutting down the external distractions, let's learn to rewire our brains first to stop overthinking so we can shut down the biggest internal distraction of all.

- **Embrace Uncertainty** - Overthinking happens because we worry about the things we can't control. The uncertainty makes us nervous, and when that happens, our brains kick into overdrive and start running through multiple scenarios thinking about everything that could go wrong. Things are not always going to work out the way you want it to, but overthinkers tend to dwell on the questions that they cannot answer. There will be things that you will know and can know, and there are things that you may never know or come across. Rewire your train of thought and keep telling your brain that it is okay not to know the answer at all.

- **Think About the Bigger Picture** - Each time you overthink, stop and ask yourself what this is doing for you. What it's doing *to* your ability to focus. There are more important things to focus on than worrying about the "what ifs." You could spend hours, days, and weeks worrying and overthinking, and it will *still* do nothing to change the outcome. What will change the outcome? *Learning to focus.* Rewire your train of thought and start thinking about the bigger picture instead. With each worrying thought that comes, ask yourself *"Is this worry worth my time?"*.

- **Don't Make It A Habit** - Getting stuck in your head can quickly develop into a bad habit (if it hasn't already) that you don't even realize you're doing it anymore. You need to start paying attention to the thoughts that you have and hit the stop button as soon as you realize you're overthinking again. Replaying events repeatedly in your mind is overthinking. Hit the stop button. Asking yourself the same worrying questions several times is overthinking. Hit the stop button. Look for repetitive patterns in your thinking that you notice start to stress you out or make you worry, that's a good indication you're doing it again, and it's time to (*you guessed it)* hit the stop button. This is one unproductive bad habit you *don't* want to keep around.

Shutting Down the Distractions for Good

Shutting down distractions is serious business, and it is time to take the following steps to minimize the cognitive disruptions so your focus can thrive:

- **Make Use of Meeting Rooms and Quiet Spaces** - This is one to keep in mind when you're in the office. Meeting rooms exist in the workplace for a reason, and it's time to make full use of them. The best way to remain focused on what you need to do is to keep the distractions to a minimum. In an environment like work where so many people are working near with one another, phones can be constantly ringing off the hook, people will be on the move walking up and down, and several conversations could be going on at once. Not exactly the most conducive environment to hold a discussion, much less an effective conversation. Keep the distractions to a minimum, go into a meeting room and close the door, put the phones away, and then get to work focusing your mind.

- **Don't Check Your Emails Frequently** - Make it point starting from right now that you're not going to check your emails until you're done with what you need to do. Check your emails before you start the task you need to focus on or check them after you're done. But don't stop in between to do it, so you avoid disrupting your workflow. Close your inbox, so you're not even distracted by the notification window that pops up in the middle of your task. Switch off your phone or set it to airplane mode, so you're not tempted by the "dings" that alert you a new email has arrived in your inbox.

- **Invest in A Planner** - Do you schedule your day from start to finish? If you don't, perhaps it's time to consider doing that to minimize being easily distracted throughout the day. When you've got a set to-do list sorted out in your planner, you're less likely to indulge in idle time when you know what needs to be done one after the other. Using a planner here would help with your distractions at work, and even during the day. The first thing you need to do is to make a list of all the tasks that you need to get done and label each task with a priority level. Include everything that needs to be done, including the smaller, more menial tasks so you can get a clearer overall picture of everything that is on your plate, which you need to get out of the way. Using a planner will help you determine exactly how much time you have to complete each assignment, and writing it down will help you clearly see each deadline that is in front of you so you can stay on top of everything that you've got going on. Don't forget to schedule in some break time, too, so you can recharge your batteries before moving on to the next task at hand.

- **Invest in Noise-Canceling Headphones** - These are going to be your best friend when it comes to blocking out external distractions. Especially when you frequently find yourself working in a noisy environment. Invest in a good pair of noise-canceling headphones that do a good job of blocking out at least 90% of the noise. As a bonus, if calm, relaxing, soothing music helps you focus better, you get to listen to those tunes through your headphones instead of the chatter and the buzz that's going on around you. If you're going to have to listen to noise anyway, it might as well be a noise that helps you concentrate and not distract you.

- **Getting Rid of Your Extra Chair** - Depending on your office setup, you might have an extra chair at your table or somewhere within the vicinity. Unfortunately, this extra chair is an invitation for a chatty colleague to come and plop down next to you and start chatting away, distracting you from your work. Shutting down distractions means you're going to have to minimize the opportunities for other colleagues to come and chat with you, even if you may not like the idea because you don't want to upset anyone. Your colleagues will understand once you explain your reasons for doing so.

- **Shut the Door -** This only works if you have one at the office. If you work from home, shutting the door is easier to do. It may not be the most welcoming gesture, but it is necessary if you want to focus your mind and block out the distractions until you're done. If you live with others at home, let them know that when the door to your office is shut, it means you need some time to focus on your work. Unless there's an emergency, let them know you would appreciate not being interrupted for the duration that the door is closed. Do this at the office, too, by talking to your colleagues and letting them know you would appreciate if they could respect your focus time when the door is shut.

- **Operate in Full-Screen Mode -** This kills two birds with one stone. It stops you from getting distracted by anything else on your computer, *and* it encourages you not to multitask too. When you go full screen, you're forced to only look and focus on whatever it is that is in front of you. Any files and folders on your desktop are kept out of view, and so are any extra tabs or browsers you may have open.

Chapter 7: Step 6 – Sharpening Attention

The wandering mind is a hard one to reel back in. As it turns out, our brains are only "in the moment" and present for only half the time that we are awake, according to a Harvard University study. The study places our average attention span a day around approximately 53% of the time we spend awake. This means that we spend the other 47% of the time zoned out, distracted, and not paying attention. No wonder we find it hard to retain focus when the mind seems to so easily wander off on its own. Zoning out during meetings, presentations, lectures, seminars, sometimes even when we're in the middle of the conversation.

Looks like technology is not entirely to blame this time since our brains alone have a hard time paying attention for long. In this case, technology only makes it worse, since our brains are wired by design to seek out new information all the time. Technology feeds into that need, which explains why we have a hard time pulling ourselves away from the tiny screen in the palm of our hands. Author Daniel Goleman explains in *Focus: The Hidden Power of Excellence* that there are two forms of distraction. One is sensory, and the other is emotional. Sensory distractions are what's happening around you, and emotional distractions are your emotions, thoughts, inner dialogue, and feelings *about* the things that are happening around you or in your life.

Your ability to focus on your task is severely compromised each time there is a distraction. When your phone beeps or blinks, when someone comes knocking on your office door for a chat, or when there's a sudden loud sound or commotion within your environment. The moment you lose your attention span, you have to start all over again as you lose your train of thought. Getting back into the swing of things might take longer than it should, depending on how quickly you've trained your ability to stay focused. It doesn't help that the society we live in today either is constantly pressuring us to do more and move faster. From the moment we wake up, we seem to do most things in a hurry, or we multitask. We're impatient, dissatisfied, restless, and bored, and the ability to focus our minds seems to be getting harder and harder to do.

Why Do I Struggle to Pay Attention?

The problem we have today is that there's too much going on. We're *overstimulated,* and that makes it hard for us to focus on one thing at a time.

- **You're Not Interested** - When you're not interested in what you do, there's no incentive to pay attention. A lack of interest actually makes it *easier* for you to become distracted because you know somewhere in your mind you would rather be doing anything else but what you're doing right now. You'll subconsciously welcome any excuse that takes you away from your task, even when you know you're going to pay for it later.

- **Poor Energy Levels** - When you're tired, you can't pay attention. It is as simple as that. Throughout the day, as your energy levels start to fade, you find it increasingly more difficult to pay attention. You find meetings held at the end of the workday feel excruciatingly difficult to stay focused on compared to meetings held in the morning. Yet, most of us don't make it a disciplined enough practice to get the adequate sleep hours we need each night, so we're refreshed and focused for tomorrow.

- **You're Emotional** - We're emotional creatures, and that's not a bad thing, but being emotional can affect your ability to pay attention when you need it most. Emotional intelligence is a subject area that repeatedly emphasizes how important it is to regulate your emotions and keep them under control so you can master them to your advantage. A byproduct of the hectic lives we lead is we spend a lot of the time feeling stressed, a negative emotion that can severely impact our ability to pay attention. Emotions tend to be powerful, volatile, and overwhelming elements on their own. When you add chronic stress on top of those all the emotions, you might already be dealing with. The physical and psychological effects can be profound, extending beyond just compromising our ability to pay attention.

- **You're Hungry** - Paying attention is hard when you're distracted by the hunger pangs that go on in your stomach. Hunger is not necessarily attributed to a lack of food either. Being thirsty gives the same signals that often get mistaken for hunger. But this can be a challenging problem to balance, since you don't want to be *too full* either, given that an over-fed brain lulls your ability to focus. Finding that balance where you're not too full or too hungry is the challenge, but it is important to find a balance that works for you, or this is always going to be a problem.

- **You Might Be Dealing with ADHD -** If you're struggling to stay focused, it might be because you're dealing with Attention Deficit Hyperactivity Disorder (ADHD). This symptom affects approximately 5% of children, and half of these children will likely carry these symptoms with them as they reach adulthood. Some adults with ADHD may not even be diagnosed properly if they don't recognize the signs and get the necessary treatment needed. Difficulty paying attention and focusing is merely one sign of possible ADHD issues. If you still have trouble focusing despite attempting all the strategies you can think of to try and pay attention better, and despite the strategies you've learned in this guide, you should probably consider seeking professional treatment.

Reigning It In

Like everything else you've learned so far about how to focus your mind, reigning in your attention when it starts to wander is going to take some getting used to. You're not going to be able to sharpen your attention right away, training yourself to reach that level takes time specifically because you're adjusting to a new habit. A new way of doing things.

- **Drink Your Water** - Besides being the elixir of life, it turns out we need water to help us pay attention to. A study by the University of Barcelona discovered that mild dehydration (around 2%) is enough to negatively impact your ability to stay focused and concentrate. A 2% drop in your hydration levels is all it takes to trigger thirst and start distracting you from the task at hand. If you know you're about to begin something that needs you to stay focused, be sure to drink plenty of water before you begin.

- **Be Curious** - Asking questions is one way to perk up your attention span. Meetings at work provide an excellent training ground for this since meetings are one of the hardest places to stay alert. Not surprisingly, the National Statistics Council found that nearly half of employees surveyed thought meetings were nothing more than a waste of time. Despite how you may feel about them, meetings are necessary, and crucial information is at risk of being missed if you don't learn to pay attention. However, a quick trick to force yourself to start paying attention is to go into it with a mindset that you're going to ask questions. As you listen to what's being said, start formulating some questions in your mind, so you've got no time to zone out.

- **Classical Music for Concentration** - Researchers at the University of Stanford's School of Medicine discovered that listening to classical music while you worked could help improve your concentration levels. These short, soothing symphonies engaged areas of your brain that helped you pay attention and listening to these soothing tones is a nice welcomed change for your anxious and stressed out brain.

- **Have a Cup of Tea** - That morning jolt that wakes you up comes from your usual morning cup of coffee, but the ability to stay alert? Well, it turns out that comes from tea instead. Black tea, to be more specific. L-theanine, a type of amino acid found in the tea, has a direct impact on the areas of our brain responsible for helping us stay alert and focused. A study carried out in the Netherlands found that those who drank tea were better able to pay attention compared to their counterparts who were given a placebo to drink instead.

- **Building Your Capacity for Attention** - Thankfully, your attention span is like a muscle that can be exercised to gain strength. Like willpower and self-discipline. Certain activities, like yoga, journaling, exercises, and mediation (techniques that have been mentioned in this guide already), can build up your attention capacity with frequent practice. These activities force you to pay attention, manage your emotions and filter the distractions, teaching you how to mindfully tune them out as your ability to pay attention for longer gradually increases.

- **Implement A Reward System** - Let's face it, we all work better when we know there is some reward waiting or us at the end of that road. That reward is motivation (sometimes we need that extra push in addition to our goals). If you knew there was a reward waiting for you once you've completed a task, you'd be more motivated to get it done and get it done well as soon as possible because you're looking forward to that reward. This strategy can now be implemented to help you build your capacity to pay attention for prolonged periods. Let's say there was a project you needed to get done within an hour and delivered back to your boss, set up a reward system at the end of it to spur you to stay on track. Tell yourself as soon as you're done committing this one hour of focus to the task; you're going to reward yourself with a nice, calming cup of tea in the break room. Your reward should be something that makes you happy, something you to look forward to and it can be anything you like as long as it works for you.

- **Getting Enough Sleep at Night** - You've seen what a difference a good night's sleep can make. The way you operate when you've slept a full 8-hours the night before and the way you operate when you've had hardly any sleep is significantly different. The first one, of course, supports your ability to pay attention. With enough sleep, you're energized, in control, and in a better mood. All the ingredients you need to pay attention better. Completely different than when you're sleep-deprived and you're irritable, moody, and so tired to the point all you can think about is getting this day over with so you can go home and sleep again.

Chapter 8: Step 7 – Stress Management

Stress can cause severe disruption in your ability to focus. When you're stressed, the simplest thing or task can appear to be something overwhelming. Your behavior might become frantic and erratic, even unpredictable as the stress piles on until you finally reach a point where you can't think clearly anymore. Being in a state of frequent emotional turmoil can lead to stress, which, as we all know, is never good for the body. The elevated cortisol levels, adrenaline pumping through our veins, these are referred to as "stress hormones," and when they course through our bodies, they're pumping us up to react in a way that is quick and strong. Unfortunately, it is also difficult to concentrate when you're in this state.

Despite what you may believe, it is not normal to be living in a constant state of stress. You may think that it can't be helped because of the pressure experienced at work, juggling family, and personal responsibilities. Or that's just how your life is, and stress is a part of it, but this is not how we were meant to live. Stress can have a tremendously negative impact on our bodies, not just physically, but emotionally too. On an emotional level, feeling stress and other negative emotions can result in irritability, feeling depressed and worthless, loss of purpose in life, and loneliness. We feel isolated like nobody understands what we're going through, we feel anxious when it seems like things are not getting any better and eventually start to feel depressed because of all the imagined worries we are carrying about on our shoulders. That's the kind of impact negative emotions can have on our minds.

Managing Your Stress Levels for Better Focus

Recovering from stress is not something that is going to happen overnight. Nor is it something that you can accomplish all in one go. Change can be difficult, so you should do it in small stages. Baby steps. Change comes easy for some, but for others, it takes a while to get adjusted. Rushing into it may make you feel overwhelmed and unable to cope. Doing too much too soon is going to make you crash and burn really quick, so slow it down and do things one step at a time.

- **Stress Balls Save the Day** - To calm your nerves in times of stress, stress balls are something you always want to have handy when you need it. If you don't have a stress ball, no problem, it is very easy to make one of your own. Simply fill a balloon with either flour, rice, or even play-dough. Don't forget to double wrap the balloon at the end to ensure that it is nice and secure. Each time you feel nervous and anxious, distract yourself by using the stress ball. Close your eyes, regulate your breathing, and keep it going until you've successfully calmed your mind enough to resume your focus.

- **Make A Stress Journal** - It is like any other journal, except this one is just for you to pour your heart out. Or rather, pour your stress out. This is the safest way to channel those stressful emotions you're holding inside in a way that is not going to hurt anyone. This includes you too. No one gets hurt with your words, you don't do something you regret, and you still get to release all your pent-up emotions by pouring them out into the pages of the journal reserved for your eyes alone.

- **A Stress-Relief Toolbox** - Having a toolbox with you at the ready filled with items that help calm your nerves can be extremely helpful when stress threatens to get the best of you. You can fill this toolbox with anything that you like. A few positive affirmations quote maybe. A personal item of yours that helps calm you down. A picture of the people you love most. Maybe even your stress ball can be kept in there. These items should serve as reminders that everything is going to be all right, and you need to pace yourself, breath, relax, and weather the storm. You've probably got a toolbox handy at home to fix any repairs needed. This time, you're going to have a toolbox to heal your emotions instead.

- **Being One with Nature** - Instead of being cooped up at home, getting more stressed by the minute and nothing gets done in the process, get moving by going for a walk to change up the environment. Exercise is a great way to improve your mood, and there's nothing like a change of scenery to take their mind off what's worrying you. It removes you from the cause of your stress, while at the same time giving you a chance at some exercise and a chance to breathe in all that fresh air. You could also take this time to observe all the beauty that nature has to offer. This could help you calm down significantly and feel much happier in the process.

- **Avoid All Negative Talk** - You've had your fill of negativity in your life with all the stress that you've been carrying around with you up to this point. It is time to put that behind you. Avoid any kind of negative thoughts completely. Negativity only serves to feed into your stress even more and make things seem much worse than what they are. If what you've got to say about yourself is even remotely negative, stop at once. Don't do it. Don't say anything at all because it's only going to make you feel even worse about yourself. Whenever you catch yourself doing this, make an active effort to turn that thought around into something positive. It'll be tough to do in the beginning, but it gets easier with practice. Think about this, every moment you spend indulging in negativity is another moment wasted when you could have been focusing.

- **Be Kind, Do Good** - Immerse yourself in good deeds to help lift the veil of stress that has been shrouding you. Because when you put your energy into helping others, you're less focused on your own issues. Nothing boosts your morale quite like the satisfaction of knowing you've done something good for others without expecting anything in return. You did it because you wanted to. Being involved in charity work or doing something for a good cause reminds you that there are other people out there in the world with bigger challenges on their hands, and it'll help to give you new perspective because if they can weather the challenge with a smile on their face, you can handle anything that comes your way.

- **Read for Inspiration** - Any book or media that emphasizes on positivity and empowering yourself and your thoughts is what you should start immersing yourself in right now. You are rebuilding yourself once more, training your mind and helping it to crawl out of the negative pit that stress has left you in. Think of your mind like you would a growing child. For it to become better and stronger, it needs nutrition. Let the inspirational books be the nutrition for your mind and soul, your way to heal. Inspiring stories help to fuel your motivation once again, and when your motivation is running full-steam ahead, it's easier to remind yourself *why* you should be focusing on getting things done.

- **Flocking Together with Other Birds of a Feather** - Surround yourself with positive people to see a transformation in your life. It's not that these positive individuals don't deal with stress at all, because they do. They've just learned how to manage it better *without* losing focus, and that's the lesson you want to take away for yourself from the time you spend with them. When you surround yourself with only people with positive mindsets, you'll slowly adapt the way you think to emulate them as their wisdom, their outlook, stories, and affirmations slowly seep into your way of thinking. Not to mention their stress management techniques. This is great for your healing process because being surrounded by all this positive energy is going to have an uplifting effect. The complete opposite of what stress made you feel like.

Taking Care of Yourself Again

Stress will always linger at your doorstep until you learn to take care of yourself again. To prioritize your self-care more often. Performing at our best with a sharp, focused mind can only happen when we take care of ourselves mentally and physically. Even spiritually. Taking care of yourself and focusing on you is going to be an important step in your stress recovery process. When you learn to love yourself and feel good about yourself, staying sharp, alert and focus doesn't feel like the struggle it once did anymore. *Because you're happier.* Use the following guide to help you take care of yourself once more and learn to love yourself again:

- **Eat Well** - Stress may have had a disruptive effect on your eating patterns. Now that you're trying to be free, you can start trying to eat well again. Don't skimp, starve, gorge, or binge. This is not a productive habit because it is going to put your body through emotional and physical highs and lows, which could result in you crashing and burning long before you should. Keep your mind sharp, and your body fit by eating a well- balanced diet that meets all your nutritional needs and steers clear of anything which is going to impact your body negatively.

- **Meditation to Heal the Soul** - One of the most calming exercises around meditation, a practice that has numerous benefits, among which include helping you regulate your emotions. Spend a few minutes in a day meditating because it is important to stop and calm the busy mind every now and again. You have a lot going on in your life, especially with recovering from stress. Meditation teaches you control over your emotions by teaching you how to deliberately slow down your thoughts through mindfulness.

- **Be Grateful All Day and Every Day -** There is the power to be found in expressing genuine gratitude for everything you have in your life, it lifts your spirits and fills you with happiness, which improves your satisfaction levels. It helps you remember and all the little blessings you should be thankful for, which can easily be forgotten and taken for granted. Practice an attitude of gratitude every day and look at what a difference it can make in your life. It can do wonders for your healing process. Perhaps that's the reason the phrase *too blessed to be stressed exists.*

Conclusion

Thank you for making it through to the end of *How to Focus Your Mind*, let's hope it was informative and able to provide you with all of the tools you need to achieve your goals whatever they may be.

Improving your focus is going to change a lot of things in your life. Your mind is your muscle, and you can train it to do anything you want it to. Work on your ability to focus by frequently practicing the steps you have gone through in this guide and commit to eliminating the habit of multitasking from your life once and for all. Some of these steps may take time to implement and get into the habit of doing, but take it slow, be patient, and give yourself time to adjust. Small steps each day eventually lead to a big improvement, and it takes 21-days for a new habit to stick and become the new norm.

Finally, it is important to remember that at the end of the day, we're only human. We do our best, and that's all we can ask of ourselves. Sometimes you may find your mind still wandering, and that's okay. The important thing is when you do, acknowledge it, and bring it back to focus on the task at hand again. The ability to focus will get better over time, and until then, stay optimistic, persevere, be patient and keep going!

Book 2: How to Rewire Your Brain

7 Easy Steps to Master Neuroplasticity, Mind Hacking, Think Habits & Practical Neuroscience

Troye Bates

Table of Contents

Introduction

Is it possible to change your way of thinking, your way of behavior? Your emotional attachment to things? Is it possible to modify who you have become?

This is a question for many because, while you may feel like you are doing your best, you may not feel successful. Or maybe you realize something is missing and you want more out of life. Or do you have an annoying aspect of behavior that hinders you. You just know that something must change. In this guide, you will find that not only is change possible, but you can take the bull by the horns and create the person you desire to be. You can create the road map to the journey you desire. No longer are you limited because of what you thought you could not do.

According to the theories of neuroplasticity, you can. You can change those things and even more. It is basically mind over matter. Your thoughts govern who you are. Neural activity helps to make you "you". Everyone is tied to their brain. The brain is not like a computer, it is constantly changing

As you investigate what neuroplasticity is and how it affects you, you'll learn it is the ability of the synaptic connections of the brain to transform and correct, motivated by an injury or some other stimuli. The significance of it on injury and rehabilitation is astounding. Change is possible because of the brains ability to remap.

Your thoughts, emotions, behavior, and environmental stimuli are aspects of the neuroplastic conversion. How much of what you do, say fell and your surroundings impact your mindset and your ability to change? Even in rehabilitation of the brain after injury there are phases of neuroplastic healing and change.

But neuroplasticity has both a positive and negative. You become aware of negative plasticity in those actions that are offensive and unproductive. The good news is it does not have to remain that way. You can redefine yourself. If you are not currently representative of the person you desire.

How do you start this change?
Get a grasp of how your thoughts impact who you are and the choices you

make. Most of what you do is by habit. You are accustomed mentally and physically to do the same routine. And if you alter things, they seem out of place and are awkward.

Because you do an activity repeatedly over a period, you become used to getting a certain response, you then anticipate that response and arouse a certain feeling. After a while your body (mind) seek or crave that emotion as a condition of that activity. This forms the sense of being restrained in this cycle.

But you can change. This requires you to be committed, dedicated and repetition to change. So, how do you initiate your transformation? Activate those elements that influence our being, the conscious mind, the subconscious mind, and the analytical mind

You are the accumulation of your past events. You relive daily your emotional connections to past events. Like your choice of people in past relationships. You know it never ends well, but you do it again and again. With the repetitive nature becomes addiction. Even to the point that you re-experience the event through your thoughts. Each time you rewind it in your mind, you re-ignite those feelings and emotions. When you remain in this cycle of repeating thoughts and emotions, it become difficult to change.

How do you cross over this point?
Your bodies defense to change is procrastinate. Being uncomfortable in this new arena of change, your mind seeks to return to the old habits. There are a variety of ways to tap into this mental change. Meditation is a technique which allows you to harness your subconscious and initiate a change. Within meditation are different approaches/ focused meditation, conscious awareness (mindfulness meditation), etc.

As you read you will see how you think influences your body. To change your mind and rewire your brain, you must be cognizant of the unconscious script that is running and begin to act with determination.

Learning how mind hacking is a way of achieving entrance to the mind. It directs the answer to how to change your mind. If you wish to make a change, you must begin by recognizing your contradictory – mentalities. Pay attention to what voices you are listening to. If it is not positive, and the question why.

Accept that no one is perfect including you. As you begin do same things, because you can grow with small goals and gain success. And tell yourself its ok to fail. Because when you give yourself permission to not be perfect and to have some failure, you also take away that pressure and allow yourself to find success.

So, how does your brain rewire itself?
The motivation needed to rewire your brain is based on your consciousness. You must work on becoming consciously aware of your thoughts. Being able to identify and be aware of your thoughts starts the process. Also identifying the emotions which line up with achievement of your objective. As you read more you will find the steps necessary to rewire your brain. In practicing the process, it is important to note that change will not occur without the repetition, determination, and commitment. Another important element is being able to visualize what you desire to change. Imagining your success, you will propel toward that goal. Let your actions match with what you verbalize. Rewiring your brain will not take place if it all does not align together. Make it a conscious act to think, feel, imagine and take action to connect with you envisioned success. You are on the path to rewiring your brain.

Is it your issue that you are struggling to enjoy life?
You can find joy in life. You can turn the page on finding your happy place. To build yourself into the person you desire to be, utilize the instrument you have, your mind. While there are so many schools of thought which offer opportunity to rewire your mind, Practical Neuroscience is based on the concept of finding and remedy of neural and mental ailments.

Your emotions trigger your memory construction; and understanding the motivation for change often can impact its success. Visualize changes in your mind. Consider how you can develop, empower and support your minds power.

Brain health is a considerable portion of the process. It is the principal and most critical element in practical neuroscience. Having proper nutrition and fuel needed to execute and function at its peak. Also, sleep is important for brain health. Just like having a physical health is vital, so is your brain's health. The brain is pliable and capable of change. And when the brain changes it influences a change in your behavior. The more you practice changes you desire, the stronger you become. It may be difficult in the beginning because your brain is used to your long-standing conduct, but it will become easier as your brain adjust to the new you.

The interaction of what you feel, what you think, and what you do, creates a stimulus and response cycle.

The battle is in your mind, as your thoughts and feelings are working in opposition of your welfare, but you must act. Initiate frequent positive action, the more you identify as the person you envision or desire, the better you will become at taking those affirmative steps in the future. Be mindful, it is never too late to change. You may have some difficulties in the process of unlearning the old and learning the new. Learn to live and act mindfully. Avoid the pitfalls of human nature to grab onto and embrace bad experiences.

Now it's time to REPROGRAM YOUR MIND

How can you change it if you do not know what it is you need to change? So, tapping into the subconscious mind is the target and the beginning. In order to learn how to practice subconscious mind power, you must identify your subconscious thoughts.

It is obvious that you are cognizant of your conscious mind, because when you are alert you are in your conscious mind. However, when you are slumbering, you are in your subconscious mind. But also, your subconscious is operating behind the scenes even when you are conscious. In other words, subconscious mind is that part which is not seen, or obvious to appearance. You may think of it as being beneath the surface. The conscious mind provides you with the capability to think, reason, process and choose, whereas your subconscious mind lingers untouched.

Your emotions, inspirations, motivations, instinctive ponderings and even divine realizations originate in the subconscious mind. You can harness the power of the subconscious mind to guide and direct you to better choices.

Learn to recognize those learned and self-doubting thoughts. Stop buying into those self-defeating images and replace with positive thoughts and images. Don't allow those negative imaginations limit your ability to succeed. If you believe positively about yourself or your capabilities, your expectation and actions will follow those thoughts and your results are what you expect.

Ask yourself why do you think you failed at the specific task?
When you silence, those negative thoughts, then you must replace them with helpful and productive thoughts. Change your outlook and approach to your objectives. When you concede your talents, capabilities and competences along with being able to be gracious in acceptance of encouraging remarks and accolades from others, you begin the process. Changes do not have to be dramatic. Learning to take small advancements and achieve small successes will give you the confidence to continue.

Learning the effects and the influences of your subconscious allows you to learn how to recognize when it is misleading you and to how to "change your mind". Be clear about what you seek to achieve. See your success, believe in yourself, and your subconscious will believe it too.

Can your conscious mind transform your subconscious mind?
Through our unconscious choices and actions, you operate in an automatic mode. If you want more, become more. But do so by transforming those thoughts which drive your emotions and choices. Don't allow your negative thoughts define who you are. The only way you can succeed is to make a conscious attempt. And it begins with you recognizing, accepting and admitting your capabilities.

Whenever you begin to think negative thoughts, counter that thought with a positive affirmation about yourself. The sky may be the limit, but, set your goals and expectations so that you can achieve and accomplish them. Transform your mind to transform your world.

Chapter 1: Neuroplasticity

Neuroplasticity is defined as the adeptness of the synaptic connections of the brain to transform and adjust, stimulated by injury, training, or activity. According to neuropsychologist Dr. Celeste Campbell, "Neuroplasticity is the brain's amazing capacity to change and adapt". The physiological changes in the brain occurs in consequence of involvement and connection to the milieu in which we are in.

During fetal development before birth and until death the brain is constantly changing and adjusting to an individual's needs. The links between cells react and restructure as a response to changes in your circumstances and needs whether change in environment, learning or injury. So, from the time of conception until you die, your brain can adjust and change in such a way to allow you to perform at different levels. This is representative of the process by which individuals adapt to and acquire new experiences.

Neuroplasticity takes an influential stand for brain injury rehabilitation. The rehabilitation of the brain involves renovating the connections between the nerve cells/neurons. The extent of the recovery of the physical and cognitive faculties are reliant on the restoration of the electrical connection. The "re-wiring" of the brain increases the potential to redevelop the ability to perform an action which was governed in an area damaged by injury and control is assumed by an alternative unimpacted portion of the brain. The cellular connectors respond markedly to this mode of transformation and growth. This is noted in cases of stroke rehabilitation. The impact of damage to a particular area of the brain hinders the ability to perform. Neuroplasticity suggests that the brain can and does recover.

Neuroplasticity also known as neuroplasticity, brain plasticity, neural plasticity. The brain has the capability to constantly change. I.e. Brain activity use in a specific utility can be moved to a different area in the brain. The size of the gray matter changes and synapses may get weaker or get stronger as time passes. The synapses is a link joining two nerve cells, comprising of a miniscule opening by which stimuluses transfer by distribution of a neurotransmitter. The objective of neuroplasticity suggests that it enhances the neural networks during phylogenesis, ontogeny, and physiological learning, as well as brain injury.

The origin and development of any living thing in organism form whether psychological (moral development) or physical is ontogeny or ontogenesis. Ontogeny begins at conception and is continuous through maturity and entire life span.

Ontogeny comprise the evolutionary record of an individual over time. Recent studies have indicated that the brain has the capabilities of being trained or rehabilitated even through maturity.

Observation of neuroplasticity is done in various microscopic levels. Observation of changes in single specific neurons or the grander gauge of modification like cortical remapping as a result of injury.

Each area of the body is linked to the brain in an area that correlates to create a cortical map. The cortical map is a symbolic representation of the motor operations in the cerebral cortex. Cortical remapping occurs when the cortical map through stimulation is altered and forms a 'new' cortical map. This is also known as cortical reorganization. After a major injury such as amputation or wound causing damage which interferes with cortical mapping and the map becomes no longer germane. In such instances, another area of the brain will take over the functions which was originally controlled by the damaged area. A neighboring section of the brain which is unchanged and receiving input create the path for the remapped area.

Other factors that influence neuroplastic change include thoughts, emotions, behavior, and environmental stimuli. These are activity-dependent plasticity. This is significant in healthy development learning, memory and recovery from brain damage. Synoptic plasticity is the single cell changes between neurons. Non-synaptic plasticity signifies variations in their essential volatility.

It was originally considered that the adult human brain was "hard wired", that it was fixed. However, in more recent years, it has been discovered that it in fact was readjusting constantly to change. There is cortical and subcortical rewiring of the neuronal circuits in response to training as well as in response to injury.

Neuro refers to the nerve cells and plastic implies the changeable character of the brain. This ability to learn and adapt is the inspiration of educators, trainers and therapists. By teaching, therapy and training, they witness and experience how individuals change by learning through repetition, practice, exposure, and concentration.

Recent discoveries show that the brain continues to change throughout the life span. At all ages the people continue to learn and transform in the brain in neural system. This has only been accepted as fact by scientist in recent decades.

It is apparent that a child's brain is extremely dissimilar to that of a mature person. While it is widely accepted that the child's mind is continuously changing, we now know that the adult mind can change and adapt as well. No longer are those born with certain disabilities and disorders constricted to these physical and mental limitations.

The remapping and reorganization of the neural system make it possible that people with brain damage caused by stroke or accidents can recapture lost functions. The brain can rewire around these damaged regions.

Neuroplasticity is stimulated by repetitive activity. The Neurons link or rejoin and alter the brain's configuration and utility as a result of the motivation created by exposure to repetitive communication or activity. Dependent on what is being acquired, this could be intellectual, sensory, or physical.

If you desire to learn a new skill such as speaking a new language repetitive inputs are needed to accomplish eloquence. The informational inputs to achieve this new skill are from sounds cadence vocabulary and grammar habitually practiced with commitment over a period of time. Repetition is applicable in learning in other genres as well. Physical stimulation and sound and the association of those sounds to the selected activity generates learning in music. And the repetition of these actions reinforces the learning. This repetition is exercising your brain.

Similar to physical exercise, mental exercise is necessary for mental health. The more you exercise your body you stretch your abilities. The more you exercise your mind; you increase brain growth. "Repeated practice can set you on an upward spiral, with the joy of the effort and the results spurring you to continue to try."

Rehabilitation of the Brain After Injury

Neurogenesis is the big word here. It is the process by which nervous system cells, the neurons, are produced by neural stem cells. Simply defined, it is Neuro, involving nerves and the nervous system; genesis, the beginning of a thing. In essence; it is the birth/rebirth. The generation of new brain cells once believed as impossible is now in fact a reality.

Research now show that neurogenesis occurs in and during adulthood. It is however limited to certain portions of the brain. Much research is given to identify the regions where new cell development occur. Also, investigations are directed to ascertain how to stimulate or constrain neurogenesis. Another part of research strives to determine how new neurons are integrated into the established functioning brain. Findings from this research encourages the hope is that it will help people recover and restore functions after brain injury.

NEUROGENESIS is the birth of new brain cells. Evidence supports the theory that neurogenesis occurs in adult mammalian brains and persists well into old age. But current research has revealed that other parts of the brain, including the cerebellum, may be involved as well. The amount of rewiring generated by the incorporation of new neurons in the formed paths is uncertain and such rewiring may not serve a functional purpose.

An unanticipated outcome of neuroplasticity is the relocation of brain activity related to a particular function. This occurs it situations of rehabilitation in cases of brain injury as well as a result of this can result from ordinary events. Neuroplasticity is the basis by which issue that supports the scientific basis for treatment of acquired brain injury with goal-directed experiential therapeutic programs in the context of rehabilitation approaches to the functional consequences of the injury.

There are stages of neuroplastic healing and change. Psychiatrist, psychoanalyst and author Dr. Norman Dodge states there are five stages of brain healing and change. He asserts that that the brain can heal disease and dysfunction.

Repair of the health of nerve cells: Bolstering nerve cell wellness is imperative in the treatment of learning disorders, autism, and dementia. Through changes to tackle food sensitivities and removing toxins.

Neurostimulation of brain cells: The introduction of stimuli to the brain promotes the development of new circuits and links. Stimulus come is a variety of ways. Whether intellectual, sensory, or physical, these exercises can stimulate recovery in inactive or sleeping cells causing the brain to develop control.

Neuromodulation: Triggers the parasympathetic nervous system which is a part of the (ANS) autonomic nervous system. Its role is to regulate homeostasis and the body's rest and digest response which is the balance and maintenance of the body's system. This establishes the structure of health, growth, and restoration.

Neurorelaxation: The brain is at its peak for learning when in a relaxed state. Sleep gets better when in a relaxed state.

Neurodifferentiation and learning: The previous two stages prepares the brain to be receptive. As the brain has been modulated and relaxed, it is more attentive and better able to distinguish slight variations in sensory experiences and to assimilate them appropriately.

Not everyone will experience all the stages of change. Most people will, experience each stage, while others depending on their circumstance may not.

In the alternative of the positive impressions of restoration of neuroplasticity, it is not always good. Just as upward spirals are built, sometimes downward spirals are developed as well. Addictions, negative thoughts and destructive behaviors are also consequences of neuroplasticity. The repetitive practices develop these results. What we consume physically, sensory or intellectually influences what we think and how we act.

Negative plasticity causes offensive and fruitless actions and thought patterns. However, these negative habits can be unlearned and replaced with positive one. Learned behaviors can be unlearned.

Redefining Yourself

Redefining yourself suggests that the you that presently exist is not the you that you would like to be. Whether it is you are not being your best self and reaching the potential you desire or whether you seem to repeat the same destructive behaviors. When you desire to change the person who presently reside inside of you, you are seeking to modify some aspect of your personality. The question is how do you institute the change? It starts in the mind, your thought processes. You have probably heard many times "So a man thinketh so is he." Is it true, that you are controlled by your thoughts? This not only comprises the complete human existence, but it is also reflective of all aspect of his experience. "You are the sum of all your thoughts.'

Understanding how your thoughts impact your being is the beginning of transformation. We all function in a habitual system. When we get up in the morning, usually it is about the same time, we have the same routine getting dressed and prepared, we drive the same path to work daily, see the same people every morning, and has the same ritual for most of the day. So, we have conditioned our mind and body for the same routine. And when things change and are out of order, we become uncomfortable.

By the time we reach our 30's we are pretty much who we are going to be. We are approximately 95% of who we will be. We function in an automated state acting with behaviors that are remembered and done without much thought. These behaviors have emotional reactions based on mechanical habits, viewpoints, ideals and opinions, that performs as if it was a computer. So, redefining yourself is like deciding which program to run.

Neuroplasticity illustrates the ability that you can rewire your mind by creating new learning experiences. It also shows that it applies to a variety of circumstances and situations. It is not limited to neurological disorders and damage from injury, but also when you need to unlearn behaviors and even addictions. By retraining your brain and changing habits, you can rewire you mind and create new habits and behaviors. When you repeat the same activity repeatedly, there is an emotional response associated with it and your body responds and you feel a certain way.

It is like the experiment by Pavlov and his dog. Every time he would ring the bell, he would feed the dog. And because of the anticipation of the food, the dog would salivate each time he heard the bell ring. We are the same way. If you do an activity or interact over and over again and you get a certain response, you have the anticipation of that response and it evokes a specific emotion with in us. This can be good or bad. But because this is a habitual action, we continue to repeat those habits and keep having the same emotions. And when we do not, our body (mind) seek or crave that emotion.

This creates the feeling of being locked in your circumstances. You seem to keep going through the same things yet again. You do not have to be stuck in your current state of affairs; but it will take work. Commitment, dedication and repetition to change is required.

How do you initiate your transformation?

There are three active players that influence our being. Our conscious mind, subconscious mind, and analytical mind. Our consciousness is that which we are aware, and our subconscious is that which we are not. Our actions are on automatic. We do things and feel emotions without conscious thought. But our subconsciousness is operating based on cues from us. Our analytical mind separates the two. Using our analytical mind, we can begin to take control of our circumstances.

The theory that we influence our subconscious mind through focused effort. This is where meditation comes in. Through practical application of repetitive techniques to focus, we slow down thought processes of our mind. We can then begin to alter the operating system of our mind. You do not have to wait until there is a major catastrophe or dysfunctional occurrence, but rather make a move for enlightenment or inspiration.

We claim to be the person we are because we are the sum of our past experiences. So, whatever has happened to us throughout our life, that is who we are and become. All things added together, we relive daily our emotional connections to past events. Not always conscious remembrance, but subconscious emotional response. We feel the anxiety of unpleasant memories, and in its own convoluted way, it is also a comfortable familiar. Why do we choose the same type of person, when we know it never ends well, but we do it again and again?

Looking at it from a genetics perspective, how do we become this way? If we take an event which occur in our past and investigate, we can see how it impacts our body -the subconscious mind. When we encounter a stressful or excitable stimulus, our body and brain receive a burst of power. As often as these events are repeated, your body and brain become accustomed to it and is addicted to this euphoria. So, we repeat similar situations in life to create that same response each time. Each time you do what is needed to create that emotional rush, you reaffirm it.

We also reaffirm this even when we do not actually perform it. By thought and memory, we relive the same event and evoke the same emotional and chemical response. We are sending the same signals to the brain and body as if it were actually taking place. The body being the subconscious, mind does not comprehend the difference in the emotions created from actual experience and the emotional response from the memory.

Because your body and mind are in this repetitive cycle of thought and emotions, it if difficult to change this cycle, to stop making the same choices over again. Whenever you choose to do things differently, it becomes uncomfortable. Your body and mind have anxiety because it is operating outside its normal expectation. We become 'hard-wired" when we continue to do the same thing and re-enforce those emotional cues. So, as we adventure to change, the thought processes begin, these thoughts will evoke and emotion, which then triggers anxiety. How do you cross over this point? Because your mind is now telling your body to be concerned. This is the discomfort when you begin to change.

As you enter this dominion of change, you are relieved of the sensitivity of struggle, and no longer experience the misery or the awkward emotions or embarrassment. No more murmuring, grumbling, justifications or apologies for being who you are. The procrastination factor of change is the body trying to be defensive. Because the body is experiencing a no man's land of sorts, it desires to reconnect with the familiar. So, it will encourage you, by thoughts in the mind, to start tomorrow.

You have all manner of thoughts that remind you of who you "are" and "why" change may not be a good idea for you. If you acknowledge and accept this message from the body (the subconscious mind) you will repeat the same behaviors and emotional processes. This process will cause you to image the worst possible situations. Have you ever thought about a hypothetical situation or conversation and imagined every aspect of it and the possibilities of outcome and as you continued in thought it aroused emotions in you that may have been appropriate if the circumstances were a real occurrence? But it created these real feelings in a totally unreal event. This is the effect of such emotional reminders of memories of past events.

Focus Meditation

Focused meditation is being in the present moment while maintaining concentration on one thing tuning off outside influences. It is different from the classic meditation in that instead of focusing on nothing to maintain concentration in the present you are focused on that one thing to do the same. Usually it is a sensory value like your own sensations of breathing, tastes, sounds, smells etc.

How do you practice focused meditation?

You should begin in short periods of time and increase gradually until you grow in endurance. There are a series of steps to utilize in order to begin.

1. First choose a point of focus,
2. Find a comfortable pose or posture
3. Start focusing on that central point, don't think about it experience it.
4. Constrain your internal voice. Keep it focused on that one point.
5. Don't let your mind engage you in thought. Do not allow other thoughts to interfere.

These are steps to initiate focused meditation. Meditation does not happen automatically. It requires dedication and commitment. It takes practice again and again. So, don't stress over it. Give it some time. When you start in short spurts, a few minutes at t time. As you conquer this in small events, you can begin to increase gradually. It becomes easier and easier and you become more confident and successful in your activities. Choosing the right time can also be effective in developing your practice of meditation. Morning meditation could be useful in preparing you for your complete day, while and evening meditation could be beneficial for ending your day.

Conscious Awareness

Daily we practice conscious awareness in three ways:

- Body-physical sensations
- Environment – spatial surroundings - people, places and things.
- Time – sense of time duration.

Internal concentration is a means of acute self- introspective inspection, can lead to being so deeply submerged that your attention is totally separated from your body and your environment including notion of time.

The brain in this altered state now has the capacity to exclude provocation or excitements initiated from the body or the milieu. These inducements could be from the body and the environment, as well as the consciousness of time. This capability to render our thoughts more tangible than everything else is what permits you to initiate the rewiring of your brains and change your life.

Spontaneous Remission

Is the extemporaneous healing or recovery of a disease or injury which usually advances or grows? Remission is the deficiency or nonexistence of indication or symptoms of a condition or disease under treatment. It is the complete resolution of a previously established illness.

Similarities of those who experience spontaneous remission
A Faith in the ability of a Supreme Being or Intelligence within that gave life and could heal/

A common thread shared by all who have experienced spontaneous remission credited the belief of a superior intelligence that resided on the inside of him or her. It did not matter how it was defined. Some were centered on the power of the subconscious mind, others credit the spiritual, and some in a divine healing. They believed in the power of this superior entity.

The power of the superior intelligence, the subconscious mind or spiritual nature are more impactful than the customary answers of medication, rehabilitation or care and anticipate our acquiescence to purposefully perform.

How you think forthright is influential to your body
Elements of our consciousness that impact our body and healing is based on how we think. This becomes the basis for which individuals applied and practiced intentional moderations in their mind, body and private life.

Psychoneuroimmunology is the scientific term used to express the study of the impact of the mind on the health and resistance to diseases. It investigates the correlation or link connecting the mind and the body. As a result of your thought process, you produce a chemical response in your brain. And your brain sends indicators to your body coordinating your thoughts and feeling as a response in your body.

In order to interrupt the succession of the unconscious thought it requires determination. By means of deliberation and self-retrospect, we become cognizant of the unconscious script. We eventually gain power over our thoughts. This new-found strength and power of mind and thought can regenerate and renew their health.

Self-Reinvention

When faced with uncertainty, those who experienced spontaneous remission did so as a result of a deliberate choice to make themselves whole again. No matter what the source of the ailment, a mindful resolution was made to repair what was broken.

By changing their routine, sequestrating themselves, for time to think, consider, self-examination and speculation about their desire and aspirations. Using this time to identify their future self and how to be the better person. How to eliminate guilt, suffering, sadness, selfishness and all that holds them in this loop. Consequentially, as they looked at opportunities for a nobler state of being, they also discovered new methods of assessment. Releasing old habits of thought, they accomplished a more progressive impression of who they could be. Persistence in activation and practice of their new ideals to become the newfound contemporary refreshed revitalized being. They essence become a new person with new habits. They have broken the old mold and created a new self.

Attentiveness

To develop the skill to be attentive as to lose track of time and space, you must possess substantial determination. The desire to achieve this level must be your primary focus for you. Former habits, activities, your usual agenda are eliminated. Otherwise, uninterrupted habitual activities just perpetuate the problems or illness. Dedicated to change and to recreate themselves are necessary. It is imperative and requires great devotion to the effort. No other thoughts can influence them other than their focused intent. This state of mind is not easy to achieve. The more you practice being attentive to your thoughts, the better you can become. It improves your outlook and perspective of your potential outcome.

As you become so attentive in your thoughts you are focused on your present moments, and on your intents, and you can lose track of body, time and space. The only thing that becomes real is your thoughts.

Chapter 2: Mind Hacking

Mind Hacking refers to the method of executing a feat which achieve entry to the central structure of the mind through transcendent techniques. Mind hacking is often identified as brain hacking. And is recognized as "mind over matter", suggesting that you must develop self-control. Develop practices that permits you to reach your limitless mental potential.

Metacognition

Discernment and knowledge of a person's own thought developments. Meta is self-referential and signifies as meaning in excess, and cognition is defined as knowledge, thought or understanding. Metacognition is therefore "cognition about cognition", or "knowing about knowing". Appearing in a variety of ways, it encompasses the comprehension of learning tactics as to the how's and when's of application to solutions. The major factors of metacognition are knowledge and regulation concerning cognition.

Study skills, recollection proficiencies, and aptitude to observe acquisition of knowledge are a part of the thought processes of Metacognition. It is the personal cognitive progressions and comprehension of how to direct those practices to get the most out of learning.

How Do You Change Your Mind?

Agree that you need to change how you think. When you repeatedly experience the same disappointments repeatedly, and you question why. It is hard to look internally as the place we need to change. If you are not achieving your goals and the process is repetitive, consider that it may be a result of your own thinking.

Recognize your contradictory – mentalities. These are the mindsets developed over time from previous relationships experiences and occurrences. And if these mindsets are not generating the outcomes you desire, then they are contradictory. These are usually the defeated attitudes that comes with fail attempts, such as negative thoughts and self-doubt. The contradictory thoughts appear often and unrehearsed in our subconscious. It is the thought that remind you of your inadequacies. It causes you to pause before you attempt a new thing or challenge. It is such a part of who you are, you are not aware of its existence.

<u>Start paying attention to those thoughts.</u> Observe the inner voice citing disapproving thoughts and be aware of how often it occurs. Eventually, you'll discover that your restrictive thoughts are triggered by certain topics, situations and experiences. Acknowledging this is a key component since you cannot modify that which you do not believe exist.

<u>Do the opposite.</u> Now that you know how you mind processes its thoughts, do let them interfere with your agenda. Change you discouraging reflections to encouraging contemplations. Negative meditations and positive meditations cannot reside together.

<u>Know your reasoning.</u> This involves taking measurable steps. Begin with one goal and as you accomplish it, it gives you the encouragement to keep progressing. Using the "why" technique, you must write in your own penmanship on paper, why it is important to you. This becomes your inspiration.

<u>Inspiration and Determination are insufficient.</u> While you may be driven and inspired, it takes more to meet your goals. Your inspiration may get you started but will not sustain over time. Your determination like willpower may not begin to dwindle as you continue.

<u>Understanding that it takes more that buckling down and pushing through with determination to realize your goal.</u> What is important is to accept that nothing or no one is perfect. You can have setbacks, but it does not alter your goal. You are emotionally liberated and with positiveness can attempt it again.

<u>Begin minimal and become progressive.</u> Achieving small goals and growing progressively allows you obtain positive feedback and re-enforcement. To make an enormous change, it always starts with the small steps repeated over and over. To get it started, your small goal is just the least that you'll do, but you have the option to do more if you like. For example, if you are setting a goal to become more fit. You set a goal to do at least one sit up per day. And every day you try to do "at least" one sit up. But on day you feel up to you do as many as you would like. And on other days you do the minimum, and you are still accomplished because you still met your goal. By continuing with

small goals, you create new habits and it generates positive progressive outcomes.

Don't be afraid of failure. This is a reminder that change is tough work. Understanding this helps you to adjust your attitude and grow more confident. When you encounter obstacles, do quit, but rather look for comments or suggestions and modify. By giving yourself consent to have failures, you relieve the pressure of having to be perfect. Learn from your mistakes or flops, then amend and continue progressing.

How to Get Your Brain to Rewire Itself?

The motivation needed to rewire your brain is based on your consciousness. You must work on becoming consciously aware of your thoughts. Because your thoughts influence your subconscious emotions and direct your actions. This mechanical process starts as a caution signal to the body, but often becomes a stop sign. There is a chemical reaction released in the brain set off by your thoughts. And as often as you have these thoughts and these chemical responses, the faster and stronger they become. To break this cycle and institute change – rewire the brain, you must take a series of actions.

First, Identify the beliefs that support your intentions. Know those points and principles that apply to achieving you goal.

Second, Accept your feelings and sentiments. Your emotions stimulate, charge and motivate your success. Devoid of emotion, your thoughts are detached, it has no substantive force. If there is no emotions attached to your words or thoughts, it will not mean anything. Identify those emotions support the realization of the objective. Why is this important? Invest time to experience these feelings as you concentrate on your objectives.

Next, Visualization of your success. Picture this! When you imagine you in the position of success, you will press forward toward that goal. Because the brain does not realize that it is a vision and not real, it will create the same emotions and chemical response as if you actually performed it. You can now reinforce the possibilities of doing it successfully. Create images that line up with your vision of success and practice this vision often. This will empower you to actually complete it.

Fourth, Act on it. It is one thing to dream about it, and another to talk about it. But none of it mean anything if you don't act on it. What you do must line up with what you verbalize. Rewiring your brain will not take place if it all does not align together. Associate activities that support with your ideals and reactions.

<u>Finally, Let's do it again.</u> To rewire the brain, it takes repetition. If you want to create a change, not an activity, you must repeat it consistently. If you do it occasionally; it's just an activity. But if you repeat it and do it often you create a pattern, and then a habit. Keep it going and you develop a new behavior. You have now changed your mind.

A study was done to ascertain how many repetitions were needed to form a habit. The study using 96 participants to learn a new habit like eating a piece of fruit with lunch or working out daily. Each day they were asked how "automatic" their actions felt. The findings were that it averaged at 66 days. It took 66 days to reach the point of creating a habit. So, be encouraged, be consistent. Interestingly, missing an occasional day did not impact or hinder the success of creating the new habit.

Make it a conscious act to think, feel, imagine and act to connect with you envisioned success. You are on the path to rewiring your brain.

Finding Happiness
<u>Inquire within for opportunity for improvement.</u> Ask yourself If there is one thing that you can change that would make a large impact on you. Find, that one <u>thing that you feel you need to change.</u> Then develop a deed which you can do to initiate change. For one month do it regularly. The act of working on an improvement can make you feel better even if the accomplishment is negligible.

<u>Know what you want.</u> An element of discovering enjoy in life is acknowledging what it is you really want. Imagine what the model day would be. Record it on paper, be detailed. Write every aspect and incident. This identifies what is dissimilar of your present and what you desire. Contentment is the disparity connecting hopes and actuality.

<u>Create moments for you and leisure.</u> This is time set aside just for you. Find some me-space. A little time where you are not covered with others concerns. Try to create a guilt-free moment for you. This is crucial not just for your

happiness. How you feel impact those you care about. Sanction your own take it easy periods.

Discover new things to do and places to go. Doing something new stimulates new memories and create feelings of joy or happiness. So, explore and try new sceneries, new sites, exciting adventures.

Learn to be thankful. When you learn how to be thankful, you also learn how fortunate you are. You begin to see the glass half full instead of half empty. This in and of itself will improve your emotional status. Being grateful also you to express thanks for those things both desired and not-so desirable. Being in a thankful place, alters those moment of being self-absorbed and create moments of enthusiasm.

Find incidents of joy. As often as you can find opportunities to enjoy. Finding joy is often doing simple things. Whether you find a nature trail and take a hike. Or sitting of the edge of the lake enjoying a cool breeze and taking in the scenery. The action should be something that brings you happiness. And do it as often as you can. It should be an activity that you integrate as a part of your life, not to suggest in excess.

Socialize and be active. Interact with others. It is important to be around those who are uplifting. Human nature is to socialize and interact with others. Being active will help to improve your temperament in several ways. The chemical release in the brain because of the exercise, and the interaction creates moments of interests, and simply doing something you enjoy

Declutter your life. Having a clean space will help you be happier. It doesn't have to be immaculate, but less encumbered surroundings will help.

Be Inquisitive. Having a desire to learn and do more creates and energy and intrigue. It empowers you to desire to learn more. When you are curious and seek information, then discover it, it prompts moments of joy at your success.

Don't compare yourself to others. Everyone is different and traveling a totally different path. Each has its own gifts and talents, strengths and weaknesses. Do your best and no one else's.

Chapter 3: Practical Neuroscience

Neuroscience is the methodical study of mindfulness which has amplified greatly in recent years. It has aided in establishing mindfulness' significance for well-being, and imparting acumen into the processes by which mindful guidance fosters beneficial effects.

Neuroscience is inclusive of both genetics and environment and how it interrelates to form our brains and impact our conduct. Through our experiences we alter the brain. The plastic nature of the brain allows it to be influenced and changed. The pre-frontal cortex is linked to our emotions and memories. These emotions are created by who we are physically, our response to environmental stimuli, and our cultural upbringing. However, our memories are not always accurate. Our memories change each time we educe them. Our senses can also influence the memory, such as having heard a sound when you experienced an incident, may alter the memory. Sometimes the memories are altered consciously or subconsciously to enhance or recreate our past.

Your emotions trigger your memory construction. These neural processes are interrelated. When your emotions are awakened, a signal is sent to alert memory. These activities are associated with the amygdala when triggered by your emotions, regulate the memory.

Understanding the motivation for change often can impact its success. Some seek change because of past failures, some for self-improvements, and other because of relationships. Whether it was from your past as a child or as an adult, your relationship can influence the need for change.

Visualize changes in your mind. This will initiate the areas of the brain to learn. The brain cannot distinguish between doing it and thinking about doing it. Imagining the new you may cause you to change and create the better you.

Brain Health

Brain health is the principal and most critical element in practical neuroscience. Because your brain is an organ much like the other life sustaining organs, you must take care of it. The brain is the regulator/manager and collects data. So, it is important to provide care and nutrition.

The brain needs the proper nutrients and fuel to execute and function at its peak. Consuming healthy food provides your brain with these nutrients. Just eating, is not sufficient, because eating junk food harms the brain. Sugar is especially bad.

Sleep is also important for brain health. It enhances brain function and encourages advancements in learning, creativeness, and learning. Receiving a sufficient quantity of first-rate sleep is necessary for mental health.

Your physical fitness has significant implications in brain health, enriching almost every measurable attribute of brain function.

Your brain health and function can improve as a result of hobbies or interests like recreation and meditation. Other behaviors, for example persistent multitasking and excessive screen time, can be destructive.

The prefrontal cortex is the part of the brain which executes decision making and determination. It is most vulnerable to sleep-deprivation and hunger but benefit the most from physical exercise and meditation.

Behavioral Change

The brain is pliable and capable of change. And when the brain changes it influences change in behavior. Behavioral change is probable as a result of a new mindset. The brain being a vibrant part of the body that is adept to generate growth of new neurons. The growth neurons initiate rewiring in consequence of new intellectual data and new behaviors.

Your brain needs exercise. Just like muscles the brain gets stronger the more you use it. Its composition is quite different; the cellular and its function than that of muscle. However, you must use it or lose it. The more you practice changes you desire, the stronger you become. That implies that any facet of your mind can be enhanced. Meaning, if you want to improve in a certain area, work on it. Exchange those old ideals for a new mindset. Develop a mindset for growth.

No matter what it is, you have room for growth. Whether small issues that you desire to change, or deeply entrenched destructive behaviors like substance and emotional dependences can be transformed. It may be difficult in the beginning because your brain is used to your long-standing conduct, but it will become easier as your brain adjust to the new you.

The premise that "actions speak louder than words", also apply to your thoughts. The interaction of what you feel, what you think, and what you do, creates a stimulus and response cycle. Don't let your thought take the lead, you can take control of this cycle and direct the path of your life.

The battle is in your mind, as your thoughts and feelings are working in opposition of your welfare, but you must act. Initiate frequent positive action, the more you identify as the person you envision or desire, the better you will become at taking those affirmative steps in the future. Progressive movement forward decreases the dependence on iron will as you develop new habits. This results over time as behavioral change.

So, if you want to change behaviors, it will take practice. And you should not be hindered by your age. It has been established that neuroplasticity, the elasticity of the mind continues in all ages. Be mindful, it is never too late to make a change. Pursue those opportunities that challenge you, because the fight strengthens you.

Learning

Trying to learn something new is difficult. But unlearning, and relearning is extremely hard. However, it may be complicated in the onset, the more you push through you encounter less resistance. In physical therapy, you are given a few exercises with repetition and you do those exercises each day. And gradually, you increase the repetition over a period. As you continue this regime, you become stronger and the disability you were experiencing decrease. The concept is the same in the workings of the mind. The mind needs repetition, otherwise what you have gained you may lose. In learning it is important to write it down, practice, practice, and repeat.

The default setting of the human brain is to forget almost everything we encounter, so if you want to remember something, you'll have to convince your brain to care. This can be done through spaced repetition, making written product, and taking practice tests, among other active studying techniques.

You'll be more creative and better at problem-solving if you manage your cognitive load. (This means write stuff down!) You'll also want to tap into the power of your unconscious mind to figure things out by taking real breaks. The best way to facilitate this is to remain in airplane mode as much as possible.

Psychological Health

Finally, practical neuroscience can also help improve your mental health and happiness.

By nature, our brain grasps and hold on to bad experiences. But it does so as a protective mechanism. It reminds us to be cautious. However, it can become crippling, so you must learn how to neutralize this propensity. Concentrate on making positive change and make purposeful choices and keep a journal. Practice balancing your attention and consciousness. You must learn to live and act mindfully. Don't be influenced by exterior environmental prompts. This triggers the survival impulses and fears. Meditation is a tool that helps to keep you grounded in your growth.

You only get one brain for your one precious lifetime, so knowing a thing or two about how it works is a good idea. Applying the principles of practical neuroscience doesn't require a degree from MIT; anyone can do it. And your brain and, really, you will thank you for it.

Chapter 4: Reprogramming Your Mind

You are cognizant of your conscious mind because when you are alert you are in your conscious mind. However, when you are slumbering, you are in your subconscious mind. Yet you are aware of the existence of the subconscious mind, but do not know any more than it exists. Can you describe or explain what it is or how to subdue it? The strength of the subconscious mind is a remarkable associate, if you can conquer it. Otherwise it can guide you into area of especially if you are able to master it and if it remains untamed, it can direct you into circumstances that may not be pleasant.

The Subconscious Mind

The subconscious mind is that part which is not seen, or obvious to appearance. You can describe it as being beneath the surface. The conscious mind provides you with the capability to think, reason, process and choose, whereas your subconscious mind lingers untouched.

The subconscious mind operates your conscious mind and is a warehouse of your ideals, fantasies, feelings, and views. It is an essential fragment of your brain housing your mental imprints and your unconscious decisions are made. So that when you make a conscious choice, it draws information from your subconscious mind to empower you to make a knowledgeable decision.

Your subconscious mind is the origin of emotion, inspiration, motivation, instinctive ponderings and even divine realization. Is it possible to use your conscious mind to alter your subconscious mind? Is it conceivable that such an action could can render observable transformation? To obtain a more out of life, you must believe you are empowered to achieve it. Simply by turn, in other words, if you want more of something in life, be it more money, better opportunities, greater job prospects, you have the power to make it happen. By shifting your way of thinking and by accessing the potency of the subconscious mind, you can discover a more meaningful, productive, joyful and accomplished life.

Author Yvonne Oswald, states that the subconscious mind:

"Can remember everything.

Activates the physical body.
Stores all the emotions in the body.
Preserves all your genealogical instincts.
Connects you with the divine.
Creates and sustains repeating patterns.
Makes use of imagery, symbols and metaphors.
Accepts information both literally, as well as personally.
Takes direction from your conscious mind.
Avoids processing negative commands."

Use the power of subconscious mind methodically and knowingly to influence and guide you to make the right choices. This is done by connecting with your subconscious mind. Cause it to reason, through questions, challenges, and objectives, requiring it to search within for resolutions and remedies. Meaning you can use the resources within your subconscious mind to reach the potential you desire. You cannot just erase the bad stuff, but rather you must overwrite those unconstructive notions with those of ambition, and optimism. By applying methods to channel the strengths of the subconscious mind, you will be able to reach optimistic objectives.

Being able to recognize those learned and self-doubting thoughts as limiting to your ability to act and accomplish the objectives that you're qualified to do. These thoughts of doubts will lead you to a path of disappointment. These reflections of defeat are not a true representation of the person within, but rather a rehearsal of the negative thoughts. False imaginations of doubts appearing as real possibilities that can only be proven false by your positive reactions.

If you believe negatively about yourself or your capabilities, your expectation and actions will follow those thoughts and your results are what you expect. To alter this process, stop and investigate why you are having those negative thoughts.

Why do you think you failed at the specific task?

You will probably find that those doubting thoughts are baseless. Nothing beats a failure but a try. If you don't attempt it, you will not know if you can do it. Test yourself, be experimental, do not assume anything before finding out information and trying it out.

Be positive, it will help you in your adventure. Your success in it depends on your belief in yourself and your capabilities. When you silence, those negative thoughts, then you must replace them with helpful and productive thoughts. When you concede your talents, capabilities and competences along with being able to be gracious in acceptance of encouraging remarks and accolades from others, you begin the process.

It should be a constant consideration that you just as every person in the whole world, has your own strengths, abilities and talents. Don't focus on what you can't do or where you are weak but recognize the power you do possess. Be positive

Change your outlook and approach to your objectives. Think about what it is you would like to do. Have realistic expectations. Not that you shouldn't dream big, but also consider the real expectations in terms of time and achievability.

Stop following your old routine. Because your subconscious mind operate based your old habits and routines and repeats much of it in automatic. When you are trying to change your mindset, change things up and require you mind being altered. This interruption will make the brain become active and alert. It cannot rely on the old information.

Changes do not have to be dramatic, But the little things you do can have a major impact. You are forcing the subconscious mind to connect with your present surroundings.

Be receptive as your opinions and views will change as a result of your acknowledgement of the influences of your subconscious. The effects of the subconscious motivates your interactions with your surroundings. Learning the effects and the influences of your subconscious allows you to learn how to recognize when it is misleading you and to how to "change your mind"

When you know what you want, understand "just knowing "it is not adequate. In order to achieve your goals, you must access the strength of the subconscious mind. You must also have a distinct and unambiguous idea of your objective. Be completely clear about what you seek to achieve.

Execution is the next phase. Altering the mode of thinking and giving attention to the purpose are just a portion of the process. No objective can be achieved without applying some effort to acquiring it. After you have identified your doubtful thoughts and began to rethink positive thought to replace the negatives and altered your routine to change you link to your surroundings, you should have a more positive outlook, and ready to achieve your goals.

Repetitive positive affirmations will boast your confidence. Make positive and affirmative declarations about your desires in the present tense. as if it has been achieved. Because the subconscious does not distinguished between what you envision and actuality. It will respond to that creed and inscribe in the neural pathways and modify the way you think.

You must also see it. Reinstruct your subconscious mind. As you imagine as situation, experience it as though it is factual. Allow you mind to visualize, experience and feel that encounter. Imagine a dream that you may have had that seemed so real while you were having it. During the dream your body was responding as if it was really happening. You may have awoken breathing heavy or sweating, just to realize that it was a dream. But your unconscious mind did not know it at the time and all of your emotions and feeling were alert to whatever it was experiencing in the dream state. It does not differentiate the distinction of one or the other. Positive distinct visualizations produce positive change. See your success, believe in yourself, and your subconscious will believe it too.

Meditation is a tool used to harness the brain. It requires one to acquiesce to internal tranquility. Disregard outside influence and noise. It help you to achieve your personal goals, find divine relevance and emotional stability.

Can your conscious mind transform your subconscious mind? Many believe that you can modify the subconscious with your conscious mind and alter your life. In the subconscious mind, a lot of your choices and emotional imprints are formed. Through our unconscious choices and actions, you operate in an automatic mode. Not much conscious thought is given. We recognize this process as our intuition, our inner thoughts and emotions. Some even think of it in terms of spirituality or our creative nature. Using your conscious mind to alter your subconscious begins the process of change. If you want to change something in your life, you must act. This is the conscious deliberate steps to move. If you want more, become more. Change the way you think. When you change how you think, you also empower your mind. Harness the power of your subconscious.

<u>Recognize the derogatory thought.</u> When you are cognizant of your self-deprecating thoughts, this is the beginning to your change. It has been shown through various studies, that your thoughts can have an impact on your competence. If you doubt your ability, you may alter the capabilities you already possess, simply because you doubt that you can. Failure is inevitable, because you expect to fail. Often, our own opinions of ourselves are not a true reflection of who we are. We tend to be more critical of ourselves.

Don't allow your negative thoughts define who you are. When you recognize those thoughts, PAUSE, investigate the origin of that thought and challenge its validity. Often when you look beyond that initial emotion, you'll see that there no real basis for concern. Remember the mind in the subconscious is working with memories, emotions and caution in the survival mode. Being conscious of your thoughts begins the process of change.

Nothing will beat a failure but a try. The only way you can succeed is to try. How else will you obtain the W in the win section. You have already received your L's in action and in mind. Because you continually tell yourself that you can and that you will lose.

<u>Be encouraged in your thoughts</u>. Think positively. Encourage yourself with positive affirmations. When you are trying to become stronger, remind yourself of your strength. Exchange those deleterious mental images, with productive beneficial reflections. Recognize, accept and admit your capabilities. Acknowledge that everyone (and you) is gifted with potentials, and abilities. Don't worry about on those things that are not in your wheelhouse. No one can do everything, but those which you can recognize them.

Positive Affirmation are conversations with yourself and acknowledging the good, and proficiency within. Drown out the negative with the positive. Whenever you begin to think negative thoughts, counter that thought with a positive affirmation about yourself.

<u>Amend your approach to your objectives</u>. Be realistic about your ambitions. While we may envision great accomplishments, it is also important to be realistic. The sky may be the limit but set your goals and expectations so that

you can achieve and accomplish them. Don't set yourself up for failure by setting your goals in an unattainable manner. Consider whether it is achievable, unambiguous, quantifiable, outcome determinate and set by stage or phase. Have a way of measuring your growth and accomplishment. Know what it is you want to achieve. Your goals should be accomplishable. Develop a reasonable timetable. Make sure you allow enough time; but not so much that it presents the opportunity for laxness.

<u>Altering the subconscious mindset</u>. The influence of the unconscious mind have an effect on your emotional health. Imagine how one bad incident impact your whole day. Or having a happy encounter cause you to have a lively and joyous day. Transform your mind to transform your world. The configuration of your thoughts are a result of your interaction with the outside environment and how you manage those things that impact you. While an incident in and of itself may not be neither good nor bad, but how your unconscious mind will process this event will determine your mood concerning it.

<u>Interrupt your archaic inclinations</u>. Compel your subconscious mind to connect more with your surroundings. In doing so, you engage your mind and direct it in how to concentrate on connect with your aspirations. The unconscious mind operates mainly as a result of established guides and routines from your daily living. This process creates the automatic responses you have during your everyday experiences. If it's repetitive of your normal activities, you probably give very little thought to what you do or how you do it.

In order to change the cycle, you must plug in to this subconscious cycle. Modify your daily habits each day. Interrupt the subconscious mind's routine by altering what you customarily do and prevent your mind from relying on past actions. A small change can influence your day in a big way. Switch up your schedule. Do things a little another way. This will cause your subconsclous mind to connect with your environment.

<u>Be receptive to a different mode of thinking</u>. Now that you recognize how the subconscious mind operates and impact your connection to your environment, prepare to be exposed to a fresh approach to rational and emotions. This requires time, effort and commitment, but ultimately you will realize the capabilities of brain to misrepresent an event and teach yourself to

interrupt the process of confining the outside environment to conform to your own personal assessment.

Initiate change in your life. Decide on what your goal will entail. Identify what you desire to accomplish. Don't be unclear in your desire. Be clear and defined. To be able to influence and control the subconscious mind, you must have an unambiguous ideal of your goals. Know what you want and where it is going. Don't count on chance and hopes to reach your objective, plan for it to happen. Take the steps planned to get there. Speak positive affirmations, practice and consistent, stick to the path, and drown out the negative with the positive.

Transform your power. When you know what you want, you should be ready to be committed to your goal. Your emotional strength should be poured into your aspirational goals. Your goal should be a point of focus. That in your imagination you should be able to see it as if you have already accomplished it.

Give your best toward achieving your aspiration. Put your best foot forward. To achieve your goal, you must put effort into creating the change. You may have overcome the negative thoughts and doubts, you may have even changed how you think and link to your surroundings, but it is nevertheless necessary to put effort into realizing your ambitions.

Learn how to control your mind. To build yourself into the person you desire to be, utilize the instrument you have, your mind. It is up to you to protect it, and to build it up. How you think has influence on how you live. It is imperative to identify ways to regulate your mind. Your thoughts can persuade the direction of your life by constantly repeating the same thoughts time and time again. This could lead to a fixation.

A fixation is a compulsive concern or feeling. But by harnessing control over your thoughts you can use them productively. Sometimes an obsession begins with a thought about something, and if handled inappropriately the repetitive thoughts and corresponding actions will begin to alter these thoughts and your experience and you will physically respond to this rational by developing an emotional response and you accept these new thoughts and emotional attachments as an element of your innate thinking that initiate a modification in your reasoning and beliefs. How do you harness this power of thinking?

Imagine taking that same amount of passion and apply it to gaining the objective you desire. You must learn to institute self-control. Self-control allows you to regulate and direct your mind, emotions and actions. This is a path to your accomplishments.

Meditation

Meditation is a method of training the mind. Just like exercise is to physical fitness, so is harnessing your thoughts. There are a variations of meditation methods. Each of the methods employ diverse mental skills.

One of which is focused (concentration) meditation which consist of focused attention on a distinct object. Any focal target could involve things such as watch a candle flame, your breathing, a sound or any other item you could focus on. This is somewhat difficult, but not impossible. As a novice to meditation, begin with short periods of time and build up your endurance. The simplest approach to starting meditation is just focusing on your breathing.

In focused meditation, you simply focus and refocus your attention on an objective. Each time you perceive that your mind has wandered, you refocus. Discard your arbitrary thoughts, you simply let them go. Through this process, your ability to concentrate improves.

Another practiced method is Mindfulness meditation which inspires you to monitor meandering thoughts. Do not entertain the thoughts. The idea is to know they exists. The purpose is not to intervene or be critical but just to be cognizant of them.

This process of mindfulness meditation allows you can see how your thoughts and emotions are inclined to shift in distinct repetitions. After a while you will recognize natural trend to evaluate an incident in the positive or negative. pleasant or unpleasant. Committing to a routine, an internal equilibrium is created.

Some observe a blend of both focused and mindfulness meditation. A lot of disciplines require tranquility.

To initiate your new regiment of meditation:

- This meditation exercise is an excellent introduction to meditation techniques.
- Find a comfortable position. You may sit down or try lying down.
- Close your eyes.
- Breathe naturally. Don't try to manipulate your breathing. Just breathe.
- Focus your mind on each breath and the body's movements with each intake and exhale. Observe your body actions as you inhale and exhale. Survey the changes and movements of your shoulders, chest, rib, and stomach. Keep focus on your breathing naturally exclusive of your influence. When you are distracted by thought, refocus your mind to your breathing.
- Begin with short 2-3 minutes sessions that you commit to regularly and then build up to longer durations.

Affirmations

Your mind is what permits you ponder and experience life. It connects you to the outside environment. How you see life is formed by the thoughts your mind generates. This may be unconscious to you. Actually, using your conscious mind is a conscious choice. Yes, you can decide to be actively involved or let the unconscious mind run on automatic. That means you are driven by your fears and impression of the past. If you don't want to be chauffeured by your past, dare to take the driver's seat. This is why you should use positive affirmations.

Everything started off at some point as a thought or concept in some one's mind. And because of some one's belief, effort, and action became reality. Your thoughts have an impact on your job, your family and friends, your health, your monetary concerns, and even your happiness. All aspects of your life are influenced by your thoughts. Your thoughts can be your reality. If you believe you can do something you increase your possibility for success at doing that particular thing. If you truly believe you can't do something, your negative thoughts about it will keep you from exerting the necessary effort to achieve it. Positive affirmations are positive thoughts, and thoughts Impact Your Life. Some examples of affirmations to help your change:

- I can be successful and prosperous in anything I chose.
- I deserve to be successful
- I am thankful and full of gratitude.
- When I see opportunity, I act on it.
- I find fascinating and motivating new channels to follow.
- I am structured and govern my responsibilities with competence.
- I am committed to success in all aspects of my life.
- My objectives and goals are in alliance with my principles.
- By attaining my personal victories, I also produce triumphant opportunities for others.

You can produce the reality you desire. You are empowering the prosperity and success you desire. When you let go of your old negative thoughts and begin to affirm positive thoughts for your successful future.

Chapter 5: 7 Steps to Rewire Your Brain

By having knowledge of neuroplasticity and how it shows the ability that you can rewire your mind by creating new learning experiences. It also demonstrates how it applies to different circumstances and situations. By retraining your brain and changing habits, you can rewire you mind and create new habits and behaviors. Redefine yourself. When you repeat the same activity over and over again, there is an emotional response associated with it and your body responds and you feel a certain way. You are instituting change in your life. When you do an activity repeatedly gaining that response needed to reinforce that behavior.

By activating these changes in your life, you rewrite the code in your mind. You redefine who you are and you begin to create your days. Using the methods detailed before, you become the author of your life. Determining what you desire to happen and by actions and behaviors putting them into force.

Learning how to listen to your subconscious and finding those triggers that cause you to respond in certain ways. Finding those thoughts that cause you to deny yourself in self-defeat. Ask the question why when you think negative thoughts. Don't allow you mental defense system always respond in anxious situations. Bring out the daring and accept the challenge.

Use the meditation techniques to redirect your thoughts. While you know it will not be easy and happen overnight, begin the process. Don't be afraid to start.

Focused meditation will help you to be in in the present moment. Avoid the distraction of outside influences. Focusing on just one thing like your own sensations of breathing, tastes, sounds, smells etc.

Remember starting anything does not have to be a major upheaval, but begin in short periods of time and increase gradually as you go. The steps to begin your new regime:

- First - choose a point of focus,
- Second - find a comfortable pose or posture
- Third - start focusing on that central point, don't think about it

experience it.

- <u>Fourth</u> - Constrain your internal voice. Keep it focused on that one point.
- <u>Fifth</u> -Don't let your mind engage you in thought. Do not allow other thoughts to interfere.

These are the amateur introduction to initiate focused meditation. Success will not happen automatically. Be dedicated and committed. After consistent practice, and giving it time, you will find success. So, don't stress over it. Give it some time. Once again, do not try to do it in big spurts, but rather just a couple of minutes at a time and develop into larger periods as your ability grows. This process makes it easier and easier and you become more confident and successful in your activities.

Timing is everything. When you choose the best time for your activity and commitment it can be effective in developing your practice of meditation. If you do your best in the morning, set aside a period during the morning to meditate. Or if you would rather wind down after work then maybe evening would be better for you.

You also have the option of being consciously aware. You can do this in 3 ways. That is through body-physical sensation, environment-spatial surroundings-people, place, or things, and time-sense of time duration. Daily we practice conscious awareness.

Deep self- introspective inspection (Internal concentration) allows you to be so deeply submerged that your attention is totally separated from your body and your environment including notion of time.

You can harness the power of the mind. Hack into your brain. Attain the grander scheme of "mind over matter", Develop that level of self-control. Put the practices to work for you that permits you to reach your limitless mental potential. Build up your metacognition. Empower yourself to have "cognition about cognition". Have the discernment and knowledge of your own thought developments.

How Do You Change Your Mind?

If you truly are seeking to change your mind, your way of thinking or behaving, then you must first agree that you need to change how you think. Discontinue the current journey on the cyclical path of disappointments.

Recognize your contradictory – mentalities. Know these mindsets that are developed over time from previous relationships experiences and occurrences. Don't let them produce in you do not desire. They are contradictory to your goals and objectives. The defeated attitudes that comes with fail attempts, negative thoughts and self-doubt become your heavy weights if you allow them. Start paying attention to those thoughts. *Observe the inner voice* citing disapproving thoughts and be aware of how often it occurs. Eventually, you'll discover that your restrictive thoughts are triggered by certain topics, situations and experiences. Acknowledging this is a key component since you cannot modify that which you do not believe exist.

Do the opposite. Knowing that your mind processes negative thoughts, do let them interfere with your agenda. Be in charge by changing you discouraging reflections to encouraging contemplations. Project the positive not the negative.

Know your reasoning. Use the "why" technique, Ask the question why is this important to me? What is my inspiration. Then write in your own penmanship on paper.

Inspiration and Determination are insufficient. You must act. Wanting it and being inspired is not enough. Also incorporating and accepting that no one is perfect. Being able to acknowledge and expect that there may be setbacks and that it will not alter your goal.

Begin minimal and become progressive. Take the small steps to get started. Don't be over dramatic and aim too high. Achieving small goals and growing progressively allows you obtain positive feedback and re-enforcement. Small repetitive steps will get it moving.

Don't be afraid of failure. Remember change is tough work. As with many things that are hard, you have your ups and downs. Knowing that you may encounter obstacles, prepares you not to quit, but rather look for comments or suggestions and modify. Accepting the possibilities of the setbacks, you relieve the pressure of having to be perfect. Learn from your mistakes or flops, then amend and continue progressing.

7 Steps to Get Your Brain Rewired

1. *Identify* the beliefs that support your intentions.

2. *Know* those points and principles that apply to achieving you goal.

3. *Accept* your feelings and sentiments. Your emotions stimulate, charge and motivate your success. Devoid of emotion, your thoughts are detached, it has no substantive force. If there is no emotions attached to your words or thoughts, it will not mean anything.

4. **Identify** those emotions support the realization of the objective. Why is this important? Invest time to experience these feelings as you concentrate on your objectives.

5. *Visualization* of your success. Picture this! When you imagine you in the position of success, you will press forward toward that goal. Because the brain does not realize that it is a vision and not real, it will create the same emotions and chemical response as if you actually performed it. You can now reinforce the possibilities of doing it successfully. Create images that line up with your vision of success and practice this vision often. This will empower you to actually complete it.

6. *Act* on it. It is one thing to dream about it, and another to talk about it. But none of it mean anything if you don't act on it. What you do must line up with what you verbalize. Rewiring your brain will not take place if it all does not align together. Associate activities that support with your ideals and reactions.

7. *Repeat* Let's do it again.

Its more to changing your mind. Most likely you are not in your happiest place. So, consider the simple ways in which you can find happiness.

Inquire within for opportunity for improvement. Interestingly, you always begin by looking inside. Ask yourself If there is one thing that you can change that would make a large impact on you.

Know what you want. what it is that you really want. Contentment is the disparity connecting hopes and actuality.

Create moments for you and leisure. Find that precious me-space. How you feel impact those you care about. Sanction your own take it easy periods.

Discover new things to do and places to go. Doing something new stimulates new memories and create feelings of joy or happiness. So, explore and try new sceneries, new sites, exciting adventures.

Learn to be Thankful. Being grateful is an altered state of mind. You begin to see the glass half full instead of half empty. Being grateful allows you to express thanks for those things both desired and not-so desirable. Being in a thankful place, alters those moment of being self-absorbed and create moments of enthusiasm.

Find incidents of joy. Take an active participation in looking for joy in the simple things. The action should be something that brings you happiness. And do it as often as you can.

Socialize and be Active. Interact with others. It is important to be around those who are uplifting. Human nature is to socialize and interact with others. Being active will help to improve your temperament in a number of ways. The chemical release in the brain because of the exercise, and the interaction creates moments of interests, and simply doing something you enjoy.

Declutter your life. Having a clean space actually will help you be happier. It doesn't have to be immaculate, but less encumbered surroundings will help.

Be Inquisitive. Having a desire to learn and do more creates and energy and intrigue. It empowers you to desire to learn more. When you are curious and seek information, then discover it, it prompts moments of joy at your success.

Don't compare yourself to others. Everyone is different and traveling a totally different path. Each has its own gifts and talents, strengths and weaknesses. Do your best and no one else's.

Conclusion

Thank you for making it through to the end of *How to Rewire Your Brain*, let's hope it was informative and able to provide you with all of the tools you need to achieve your goals whatever they may be.

How your care for your brain encourages the ability to rewire itself. Understanding that the practical neuroscience is based on the ideal of knowing how does the brain work. And on the finding and remedy of neural and mental ailments. Your brain health is important and requires you to use proper nutrition. Your physical fitness has significant implications in brain health, enriching almost every measurable attribute of brain function.

Because the brain is pliable and capable of change, it influences change in behavior. Behavioral change is probable as a result of a new mindset. It has it impact on learning, but the more you push through you encounter less resistance. Practical neuroscience can also help improve your mental health and happiness. By nature, our brain grasps and hold on to bad experiences. But it does so as a protective mechanism. It reminds us to be cautious.

So, if you want to reprogram your mind, start paying attention to those thoughts, and observe the inner voice that saying negative things. Be aware of how often it occurs. Eventually, you'll discover that your restrictive thoughts are triggered by certain topics, situations and experiences. Do the opposite. Now that you know how you mind processes its thoughts, do let them interfere with your agenda. Know your reasoning. Use the "why" technique. Do more than be inspired and determined. Start small and don't be afraid to fail. Learn from your mistakes or flops, then amend and continue progressing.

Harness the power of your subconscious

<u>Recognize the derogatory thought.</u> If you doubt your ability, you may alter the capabilities you already possess, simply because you doubt that you can.

<u>Be encouraged in your thoughts</u>. Think positively. Encourage yourself with positive affirmations.

<u>Amend your approach to your objectives</u>. Don't set yourself up for failure by setting your goals in an unattainable manner. Consider whether it is

achievable, unambiguous, quantifiable, outcome determinate and set by stage or phase.

<u>Altering the subconscious mindset</u>. Transform your mind to transform your world.

<u>Interrupt your archaic inclinations</u>. This process creates the automatic responses you have during your everyday experiences. Modify your daily habits each day. Interrupt the subconscious mind's routine by altering what you customarily do and prevent your mind from relying on past actions.

<u>Be receptive to a different mode of thinking</u>. This requires time, effort and commitment, but ultimately you will realize the capabilities of brain to misrepresent an event and teach yourself to interrupt the process of confining the outside environment to conform to your own personal assessment.

<u>Initiate change in your life</u>. Be clear and defined. Don't count on chance and hopes to reach your objective, plan for it to happen.

<u>Transform your power</u>. When you know what you want, your goal should be your point of focus.

<u>Give your best toward achieving your aspiration</u>. Put your best foot forward. To achieve your goal, you must put effort into creating the change.

<u>Learn how to control your mind</u> Be the person you desire to be, utilize the instrument you have, your mind. By harnessing control over your thoughts, you can use them productively.

By completing this guide, you have made your first step towards the realization of rewiring your brain. From here, you need to conduct further studies and research so as to widen your knowledge on this subject. Begin applying the tips and techniques discussed, and you will enjoy impressive results sooner than you expect!

Book 3: How to Read Faster

*7 Easy Steps to Master Speed Reading Techniques, Reading
Comprehension & Fast Reading Skills*

Troye Bates

Table of Contents

Introduction

The ability to read is, without a doubt, one of the most important skills that we require to survive and thrive as humans. Usually, we learn how to read very early in life and spend the rest of our lives, developing this skill. Typically, a normal adult can read about 250 to 300 words per minute. However, many studies have shown that with the right training and daily practice, anyone can increase their reading skills and become better at speed reading. The average reading rate of a speed reader can be as high as 1500 words per minute. Although this sounds very alluring, it is important to realize that comprehension is just as important, if not more important, than simply reading fast. It is, therefore, important for one to develop their comprehension skills along with their reading abilities.

This guide is designed to help students, as well as working adults, nurture their reading and comprehension skills to become effective speed readers. We are going to explore the art of speed reading, what it entails, and why it is important. We are also going to investigate factors that affect one's reading ability, as well as common problems that many young learners, as well as adults, face when it comes to reading. Furthermore, this guide discusses tips and techniques that one can employ to enhance their reading abilities to become a better learner. We will also look at the benefits of speed reading to comprehension and learning. Hopefully, by the end you will be equipped with the knowhow to improve your reading abilities.

All the information in this guide is drawn from extensive research, personal anecdotes, and factual data. While this guide should not be considered as a full-proof manual on speed reading, I have no doubt that you will find very practical and useful tips herein.

Chapter 1: Step 1 – Understand the Fundamentals of Speed Reading

Reading is undoubtedly one of the most common everyday activities that we do as human beings. Since reading is the primary medium through which we gather information, it is natural for us to want to do it faster and more effectively. While the average person can read only about 200 words per minute, it is possible to become faster at reading without compromising your comprehension ability. College students are typically able to develop their reading speed much easier compared to working adults. This is due to the fact that students typically spend significant amounts of time reading and analyzing copious amounts of information. Nevertheless, learning how to read first is a skill that anyone can develop with daily practice and patience.

In this chapter, we are going to discuss the fundamentals of speed reading, including factors that affect one's reading speed.

What is Speed Reading?

Speed reading is a subject that has garnered a lot of controversy over the past couple of years. While many proponents of speed reading praise it for its effectiveness on learning and comprehension, some naysayers still insist that it is an elaborate hoax at best.

So, what is speed reading?

Speed reading essentially refers to the art of reading fast, often many times faster than the average person. An experienced speed reader can typically read very rapidly, often assimilating several sentences or phrases at once. This allows them to read and comprehend long texts in a very short period of time.

Many advocates of speed reading claim that it can greatly boost IQ and improve memorization. However, some critics insist that speed reading can lower comprehension since most fast readers often fail to pay attention to absorb the information. Therefore, while speed reading is an invaluable asset that can help one navigate through copious amounts of information at work or school, it is very important not to allow speed to compromise comprehension of what is read.

Factors that affect Reading and Comprehension

The ability to read makes up only one part of literacy. In order for the text that is read to be of any practical use, it is important for one to be able to comprehend it. After all, there is no point in reading what you cannot understand. That is simply an exercise in futility and a complete waste of time. Reading comprehension is a highly complex and multifaceted cognitive process that involves numerous factors. Therefore, in order to become an effective speed reader without jeopardizing your comprehension abilities, it is of great importance that you become aware of the factors that affect reading comprehension.

Here are some of the cognitive factors that may influence one's reading comprehension abilities:

1. *Vocabulary*

The speed at which one is able to read and comprehend new information is determined to a large extent by the vocabulary they have learned. Understanding the meanings of familiar words makes it possible for readers to comprehend their relationships with other words in a given text. This, in turn, makes it easier for them to decipher meaning very quickly. An individual's vocabulary typically draws from their literary knowledge. Therefore, an individual who reads a lot of literature is more likely to have a much more developed vocabulary that one who does not. They will, therefore, be more adept at reading fast.

2. *Background Knowledge*

The amount of background knowledge that an individual has on a particular subject plays a significant role in their reading and comprehension abilities. Readers typically depend on their background knowledge to connect what they already know, with whatever information they are acquiring in the text they are reading.

Background knowledge is usually derived from an individual's real-life experiences as well as the literature that they have read. In essence, the ability to call to past memory information and link it with the text they are currently reading can help an individual become a more skilled speed reader.

3. *Fluency*

Fluency refers to one's ability to read fast, accurately, and with proper expression and pronunciation. Becoming fluent at reading is very important because it allows readers to become faster at reading while also enhancing their comprehension of what they read. It also makes them able to retain information better. Although no one is born with fluent reading abilities, fluency is a skill that anyone can develop with dedication and daily practice. As one develops fluency in reading, they spend less time trying to make out the meanings of sentences and focus instead of the meanings of entire sentences and paragraphs. This can have tremendous positive benefits on their speed reading abilities.

4. Active Reading

Most elementary school students tend to rely on instructors to guide them through certain texts. However, as they proceed to higher levels of learning like the university, they develop active reading to help them gather information on their course material. Through consistent active reading, they become skilled at speed reading and comprehension, since they are equipped with the tools of analysis, research, and reasoning.

5. *Critical Thinking*

Critical thinking abilities are very crucial when it comes to effective reading and comprehension. Readers who possess good critical thinking skills are able to interact with texts in more effectively. They are able to easily deduce the main idea of a given text as well as auxiliary ideas that support it. It also enables them to quickly draw comparisons and connections between ideas, which further enhances their comprehension abilities.

Chapter 2: Step 2 – Identify Common Reading Problems

In this chapter we will discuss common reading difficulties and how to remedy them. By the end of this chapter, you should be able to navigate reading challenges much easier.

The ability to read is something we all begin developing from a very tender age. However, many children encounter several problems when they first learn how to read. While some of these are developmental problems that may require medical solutions, others are minor problems that can be mitigated with a little training. Whatever the case, it is important to identify the problem as early as possible in order to troubleshoot them effectively. Although reading difficulties can be frustrating for a young learner as well as the parents involved, the problem needs to be addressed with a lot of tact and patience. If you are the parent of a student with reading difficulties, try and approach the situation as a natural process, just as you would go about weaning your child or teaching them how to walk.

Here are some of the common reading problems that young students typically encounter.

1. *Getting Confused by Mirror Letters*

Whereas most adults may take it for granted, many kids often get confused in identifying and pronouncing mirror letters such as 'p' and 'q,' 'm' and 'w' and 'b' and 'd.' This is something most children go through when they start learning how to read, so you shouldn't be alarmed if it happens to your child. There are plenty of learning games and tools that you can use to help your child overcome this problem. However, if the problem persists for a prolonged period, you may want to get your child tested for dyslexia, as this could be the underlying problem.

2. *Improper Directional Tracking*

Another common reading problem that many beginners face is improper directional tracking. Often, young readers are unable to read from left to right. As adults with experience in reading, we take directional tracking for granted, but for kids, this is something that takes a lot of practice to master.

In order to help your kid overcome the problem of improper directional tracking, you should practice moving your finger from left to right when you are reading with them. You should also strive to be patient with them, since learning how to read in the proper direction can take some time to become proficient at.

3. *Confusing Small Sight Sounds*

Very often, when children start to read, they may find it difficult to distinguish small sight sounds such as 'it' 'is' and 'in' due to the similar sounds and syllables. You may, therefore, find your child mixing up these words when reading passages and excerpts. This can have a detrimental effect on their comprehension if left unresolved. However, mixing up small sight sounds does not signify a learning disability. You can easily remedy this common reading problem by using word games and gentle encouragement. With time and practice, your child will naturally become more proficient at telling apart small sight sounds.

4. *Guessing*

While most children today learn to read with the help of phonics, it is not uncommon for some children to try guessing words when learning how to read. They will typically use the picture context of a particular word or phrase to guess the rest of the word, often with limited success. While it may be very frustrating to teach your young one how to read in this way, you should resist the temptation to snap at them when they make incorrect guesses. Guessing may be a sign of developmental learning problems. In most cases, however, this problem can be remedied by helping your child learn how to sound the words even if it means pronouncing them yourself at first. With your support and gentle encouragement, your child will learn how to sound words properly and become more proficient at reading.

5. *Sound Recognition*

The ability to break up words into distinctive sounds is a fundamental part of learning how to read. However, most children struggle with sound recognition. Many times we assume that as long as our child can hear the sound at the beginning of sentences, they can hear the rest of the words. This, however, doesn't always work out as we expect. Children often require months, and sometimes years, to be able to hear out and sound words properly. This is due to the fact that English vowels are often irregular. While a certain vowel may be pronounced a certain way in a particular word, the sound may change completely when the letter is used in a different word. It is, therefore, important for you to be patient with your child as they practice sound recognition when reading.

6. *Inability to Recognize Word Families*

Another common challenge that many young learners face when they start learning how to read (repetition) is an inability to recognize word families like 'mat,' 'cat, 'bat' etc. This typically slows them down as they read, since they have to single out all the letters and sound them individually. Learning how to pick out word families is important, as it improves fluency and understanding. In light of this, it is essential to support your child as they learn to identify similar chunks in words. You can help them achieve this through the use of rhyming games. This will allow your child to become familiar with similar word families, thus improving their reading and comprehension.

7. *Getting Confused by Punctuation*

Punctuations are essential to the way we read and understand sentences and phrases. However, for many children, punctuations may cause confusion and make them stumble when learning how to read. I have personally had the chance to know kids who could read words and even punctuation-free sentences very well, but once it comes to reading punctuated texts, they falter and lose track of themselves. It is, therefore, important to introduce your child to punctuation very strategically. You can begin by training them using books that only have full stops for punctuation. Once they learn how to interact with these punctuations in texts, you can proceed to introduce other punctuation marks in their literature material.

Chapter 3: Step 3 – Investigate Reading Difficulties of Young Learners

In the previous chapter, we discussed some of the obstacles that young learners typically experience when they first learn how to read. Although most of these reading problems are the natural result of inexperience, which can be remedied through practice and diligence, some of these obstacles signify a deeper underlying developmental problem.

Common signs and symptoms of learning disabilities include:

- Poor spelling ability
- Slow reading speed
- Problem pronouncing words
- Inability to recognize previously known words
- Inability to read out words with the proper expression
- Problems comprehending what was just read
- Lack of fluency when reading
- Inability to connect what was just read with previous knowledge
- Avoiding reading altogether
- Getting distracted when reading

In order to troubleshoot your child's reading problem, you need to be able to identify the reading difficulty which they experience. Notably, it may not be easy to correctly diagnose your child's reading problem, due to the fact that many of these problems manifest very similar symptoms. Nevertheless, with the right information at hand, you can accurately pick out the reading difficulty that your child is struggling with and find effective solutions. If you suspect that your child may be struggling with a reading disability, it is absolutely essential to subject them to a comprehensive evaluation, including hearing, vision, and intelligence evaluation.

Here are some of the common causes of reading difficulties that may be hampering your child's reading comprehension abilities:

Dyslexia

This is a common learning disorder that affects a child's ability to read, write, spell, and speak. Statistics show that dyslexia affects nearly 10% of the world's population, which is the equivalent of about 700 million people. Most children who suffer from dyslexia appear highly intelligent and very articulate but are unable to read properly even after attaining school-going age.

Kids who suffer from dyslexia test very highly in IQ but poorly in oral and written tests. Due to this fact, they may be mislabelled as dumb, ignorant, or lazy. As a result, they may end up feeling stupid and develop low self-esteem, which they often try to cover up for using ingenious coping strategies. Nevertheless, dyslexic children are typically very talented and creative. Some of the activities and disciplines which they particularly excel in include music, drama, sports, engineering, design, and business.

Many parents of dyslexic children tend to be ignorant of the condition, and as a result, they end up getting frustrated when their children fail to read as well as other children. Notably, they may resort to yelling to their child when they make errors, or taunt them to be like other kids. However, this only further exacerbates the problem, as the child quickly loses confidence and self-esteem.

In order to properly deal with a dyslexic child, it is essential to understand the particular traits which they exhibit. If you are wondering if your child may be dyslexic, here are some of the traits and behaviors that you need to look out for.

- They frequently complain of headaches and dizziness when reading
- They often seem to be confused by words, letters, and numbers
- Their reading and writing shows unnecessary repetitions, omissions, substitutions and reversals in words, letters, and numbers
- They are regularly complaining of seeing 'movement' on the page when reading texts
- They seem to be overly keen sighted and observant compared to other kids
- They often read words or sentences several times without understanding what they just read
- They are easily distracted by sounds
- They hear things which are not apparent to other people during conversations
- They have a problem maintaining the same handwriting and may also

have an unusual pencil/pen grip

- They can be ambidextrous or have a problem distinguishing right and left hands
- They experience difficulty in keeping track of sequenced information
- They can perform calculations but have problem-solving word problems
- They can be extremely disorderly or obsessively orderly in their mannerisms
- They usually have irregular developmental stages; for example, they may have learned to walk much earlier or later than the average child
- They have a too low or too high tolerance for pain
- They may be too emotionally sensitive and have strong moral principles
- They are more prone to making mistakes when subjected to a lot of pressure and stressful situations

While dyslexia is a common learning disability often associated with young children, the condition also affects adults. However, just as is the case with children, dyslexia in adults presents a wide range of traits, which may be beneficial or detrimental to the individual, depending on the context and their response. Some of the characteristic traits and behaviors of dyslexic adults may include:

- Choosing a job or position that allows them to mask their inadequacies easily: They will typically opt for a job where they can easily disappear in the background
- Becoming frustrated by sequence tasks
- They may decline promotions to positions which are more demanding and tasking
- They may feel overwhelmed or frustrated when expected to focus on a single task
- They may experience difficulties with standardized tests
- They may have a tendency to be perfectionists and feel very angry at themselves when they make mistakes
- They are highly intuitive and are able to understand their emotions as well as others' emotions
- They get easily distracted by noise and may become overwhelmed in high-intensity environments

- They may seem too caught up inside their thoughts such that they appear 'zoned out' to other people
- They may pronounce words incorrectly or misuse words without realizing it
- They may have an extremely good or extremely poor memory of events
- They may have difficulty remembering people's names but be very good at remembering faces
- They may have poor memory of past conversations
- They may be too self-critical and self-conscious

Adults who suffer from dyslexia typically experience difficulties when it comes to reading and writing. Some of the unique traits they may exhibit when it comes to reading include:

- They may avoid reading aloud due to overly critical self-image
- They may experience difficulties in reading unfamiliar fonts
- They may perceive 'silent' reading to be better than reading aloud
- They may adopt the use of homonyms and mnemonics to remember words, names, and sequences of events.
- Their fluency in reading and comprehension may be dependent on the subject. They will tend to be more fluent when reading subjects or topics which they are interested in and vice versa
- They may need to read and reread something several times in order to understand
- They get bored or tired when reading
- They may perceive words which are used out of context as 'wrong'

Due to the unique characteristics which dyslexia presents, most people do not fully understand the condition and may respond inappropriately to a dyslexic person. As a result, many dyslexic individuals often find it very difficult to fit in with their peers in school, as well as in their work environment. However, contrary to popular belief, dyslexic individuals are not dumb or retarded. As a matter of fact, many people who suffer from dyslexia usually end up becoming very successful in their academic life as well as their careers.

While dyslexia can greatly hinder one's reading ability, the condition can be remedied with the right approach to learning. But in order to implement effective solutions, it is absolutely necessary that the right diagnosis is made.

Typically, an educational specialist or child psychologist will perform a series of tests to determine that the reading disability is not caused by other factors such as depression and anxiety. Once a diagnosis has been made, you can work with your child's teacher, psychologist, and an educational specialist to come up with a suitable reading program. The right reading program should help your child learn how to sound out letters and words, improve their reading speed, and become better at comprehending what they read.

Some of the strategies which can help both kids and adults become better at reading faster and more effectively include:

- Reading in quiet environments with little or no distractions
- Using audio aids such as audiobooks and podcasts. You or your child can practice reading along to recorded material.
- Breaking up reading material into smaller sections which are more manageable
- Enlisting the services of an instructor or educational specialist to assess your progress and provide effective tips
- Joining a support group for people with dyslexia. This can help you or your child feel more comfortable and less alone.

Optilexia

Optilexia is a reading disability, which involves the guessing of words rather than reading them by sight. Of all the reading disabilities, optilexia is by far the most common to children, affecting nearly 70% of kids with learning disabilities. Most children typically learn to read through phonetics (sounding words) instead of guessing. However, the problem comes in when they have to read short, easy words with two or three letters. They will often resort to guessing the words instead of reading them on sight. This usually leads to comprehension problems, and may significantly reduce one's reading speed.

While Optilexia can manifest simply on its own, it often appears along with other learning disabilities such as dyslexia and attention-deficit. In light of this, it is absolutely crucial that you take your child for an evaluation by a child psychologist if you suspect they may have this reading disability.

Some of the signs and symptoms of Optilexia include:

- Frequent guessing when reading short words, but can read longer phrases and sentences without much difficulty
- Making a lot of errors when reading
- Switching up words to incorrect ones with the same first letter
- Poor spelling when reading. They may perform well in spelling contests though
- Inability to read unfamiliar words unless there is a contextual cue
- Poor comprehension ability compared to peers
- Minimal or lack of interest in reading
- Getting irritable or bored easily when reading
- Made progress initially when they began reading but then later stalled.
- Mixing up or getting confused by mirror letters such as 'b' and 'd,' 'p' and 'q' etc

Optilexia is essentially a reading problem that many children develop later in life. As a child learns how to read, they soon reach a crossroad where they have to figure out the best approach for learning new words. They can choose to either memorize them by sight or attempt to decode them. Typically, they choose the path that is easiest or one that comes most natural to them. If they choose sight-reading and memorization, then chances are they will end up becoming Optilexic.

Although sight-reading may be beneficial, and might even produce impressive results, in the beginning, complications may arise as the child begins to encounter more complex words that are not easy to commit to memory. This is why most children tend to progress very quickly early on, but then become slow at reading comprehension at around 6 to 9 years of age. This inability to progress at reading past this age may lead to self-esteem issues in the affected child.

The symptoms of Optilexia can be much more nuanced and subtle than other learning and reading disabilities. This is why most parents fail to pick them up early enough. However, if one is keen, it is possible to tell if a child is Optilexic simply from hearing them read out aloud. Very often, their spelling will be terrible, and they may make errors, which are quite simply unexplainable, e.g., interchanging entire words when reading. Adults who suffer from Optilexia may be averse to reading new material due to the challenge it presents to their style of reading. They may also feel like they are too slow at comprehension, which makes them avoid reading altogether.

While Optilexia can make reading new words very daunting, it is possible for one to correct this problem with the right reading comprehension strategies. In order to overcome their reading difficulty and improve their fast reading skills, an Optilexic needs to learn how to read by decoding, instead of sight-reading. They should channel their visual abilities and good memory towards proper phonic decoding of written texts. Fortunately, there are plenty of games and apps which can help a child learn how to decode words. With enough practice, anyone can master the skill of decoding words as they read them, hence become better at speed reading and comprehension.

Poor Short-Term Memory

Working memory is the cognitive ability to recall and use relevant information when performing a task. An example of working memory would be a child remembering the recipe for their favorite smoothie in order to make it. A number of studies have revealed that working memory plays a very crucial role when it comes to reading and general learning in children as well as adults. Children who have poor short-term memory tend to be slower at carrying out classroom tasks such as reading and computing mathematical problems than their peers with good working memory. They may also have a difficult time following instructions and answering questions in class. Older students who struggle with poor working memory may experience difficulties copying notes and listening to dictations from their instructor or lecturer. They may also take longer completing research assignments. This often leads to poor performance. Most teachers are ill-equipped on how to handle learners with poor working memory. They may wrongly label them as lazy or simply assume that they are poor at listening when, in fact, the student may be struggling to keep up.

As a matter of fact, a good memory isn't something that everyone is born with. Most people, due to genetic and environmental factors, simply have poor working memory. In order to support their disability and help them succeed, it is crucial that a child with poor memory is treated with dignity,patience, and understanding.

Some of the strategies that may help a child or adult with poor short-term memory perform better include:

- ***Educate them about their Condition***

One of the best things you can do to aid your child if they struggle with poor working memory is to teach them about their condition. You should explain to them what poor short-term memory is, what its causes are, and the strategies they can adopt to help them remember more easily, e.g., using mnemonics and homonyms. If you struggle with poor working memory yourself, there are many resources on the internet that can help you learn more about the condition and how to remedy your situation

- ***Reduce the Amount of Information you Give Them***

It is very important for you to become aware of your child's capacity if you realize that they struggle with short-term memory. If you overload them with a lot of information, they may end up remembering very little. You should, therefore, try to limit the amount of information you give them. Moreover, try summarising the most important parts of the information so that they can remember more easily.

- ***Encourage them to Repeat Back Relayed Information***

If your child suffers from short-term working memory, you can help them recall things a lot easier through repetition. Always encourage them to repeat back information before setting upon performing a certain task. If they struggle with reading comprehension, you may request them to read certain sentences or phrases several times so that they commit them to memory. This will not only help increase their speed reading overtime, but they will also be better at comprehension. You can also adopt this strategy as well if you struggle with poor short-term memory.

- ***Minimize Distractions***

If your child struggles with reading due to poor short-term memory, you may want to create a more conducive environment for them when they are practicing reading. The fewer distractions there are, the better they will be at using memorization strategies to improve their reading skills. If you suffer from poor working memory yourself, you can employ this strategy to double your reading speed and become more proficient at reading comprehension.

Reading Anxiety

Another common reading problem that affects children and adults alike is reading anxiety. This refers to a feeling of unease, restlessness, and fear, which many individuals face when reading. Often, students develop reading anxiety when they form a correlation between their failed attempts to read and the disapproval of a significant other, usually an authority figure such as their parent or teacher. Some learners may also develop reading anxiety due to past trauma. For instance, a child who has been bullied or mocked due to their accent or errors when reading may develop reading anxiety as a result. They may associate the act of reading with negative reactions and thus feel fearful of reading aloud. In some extreme cases of reading anxiety, individuals may avoid reading altogether, thereby hampering any further development of their reading ability.

Although reading anxiety is not an official diagnosis of reading difficulty, there are plenty of red flags that a parent or teacher can pick on to determine whether a child has a phobia for reading. These include:

- They often try to opt-out of reading when asked to do so, using words like 'I don't know' or 'I'm not good at this.
- They may become irritated or angry when required to read
- They may try to justify their refusal to read using phrases such as 'I can't read by myself' or 'This is boring.'

While reading anxiety may not be as pronounced as other reading difficulties such as dyslexia, it may just be as damaging to the child. If left unresolved, a child's phobia for reading can eat away at their self-esteem and make them lose interest in reading altogether. It is, therefore, absolutely essential that this problem is approached with a lot of tact and compassion. Children who suffer from reading anxiety require validation and guidance. With the right approach and support from their caregivers, they can learn to overcome this fear and start enjoying the art of reading once again.

Some of the strategies that can aid a child who suffers from reading anxiety to become more confident include:

- ***Selecting Books which Might Interest Them***

If your child struggles with reading anxiety, you can help them overcome this problem by finding books about subjects that interest them. In essence, selecting books that your child enjoys can greatly motivate them to read, hence allowing them to actively practice their skills and become better and faster at reading comprehension.

- ***Employ the Use of Graphic Novels***

Graphic novels often get a bad reputation since teachers and parents feel that they don't offer much reading practice to students. However, while graphic novels may not contain nearly as much text as regular novels, they can still be very useful when it comes to reading comprehension. The combination of texts and images allows students to exercise their analytical skills, thus allowing them to build comprehension. Since graphic novels are light reading materials, they are highly effective at remedying reading anxiety and phobia in children.

- ***Encourage them to Read Books that Have been Adapted to Movies***

Another brilliant way of getting your child to overcome their reading phobia is by encouraging them to read books that have been adapted into their favorite movies. In my experience working with children, I have found that they tend to be more engaged in a book if they already know the main plot and characters of the story. This is due to the fact that prior knowledge of the overarching concept of a book builds self-confidence and makes the experience of reading more enjoyable.

Attention Deficit Hyperactivity Disorder (ADHD)

Attention Deficit Hyperactivity Disorder or ADHD is one of the most common neurodevelopmental disorders that affect children as well as adults. ADHD typically affects learning in general, including reading comprehension abilities. Unlike most learning disabilities, which typically affect one or two areas in learning, ADHD affects every cognitive function. For this reason, ADHD is not considered a learning disability like the rest (dyslexia,optilexia, etc.).

Reports indicate that nearly 9 percent of children and 3 percent of adults suffer from ADHD globally. Often, this problem is identified in school going children due to their propensity to cause disruptions in the classroom. Notably, ADHD usually hinders the ability of a person to focus on one activity for extended periods of time. Children suffering from ADHD may, therefore, find reading difficult if they are required to focus for long periods of time.

ADHD is typically diagnosed in one of three types, depending on the symptoms involved. These include inattentive type, hyperactive/impulsive type, and the combined type.

Inattentive ADHD is a subtype of ADHD that usually manifests as forgetfulness, lack of focus, procrastination, and a limited attention span. Some of the characteristic traits of an individual with inattentive ADHD include:

- They usually fail to pay attention to instructions and end up making a lot of careless mistakes as a result
- They often have difficulty staying focussed on one task, e.g., reading, listening to a lecture
- They often seem not to be listening when being spoken too. They may appear 'zoned out' to other people
- They often fail to complete assigned tasks, e.g., homework, chores, etc. because they lose focus or end up getting distracted
- They often have problems when it comes to organizing tasks, e.g., they may waste a lot of time or produce messy results
- They usually hate tasks which involve a lot of mental efforts such as conducting research and writing dissertations
- They often seem to misplace or lose items required for normal everyday tasks such as their phones, keys, or glasses.
- They always seem to forget to do regular day-to-day tasks such as conducting house chores and running errands.
- They tend to get distracted by the mundane activities happening in their environment

Most cases of Inattentive ADHD in children usually go undetected. This is because most kids are typically very well behaved and do not cause any disruptions in the classroom. In many instances, the disorder only becomes apparent when the child constantly fails to complete homework on their own or becomes forgetful.

Early diagnosis and treatment of Inattentive ADHD are very crucial to the future of a child who is affected by this disorder. If not treated as early as possible, ADHD can be severely damaging, not only to a child's academic life but their future career prospects. It can also make them vulnerable to social problems that people without ADHD may not experience. Studies have shown that children with untreated Inattentive ADHD are more likely to suffer from mental illnesses such as depression, anxiety, and drug addiction.

They are also less likely to graduate from school and secure meaningful employment. Moreover, adults who are affected by Inattentive ADHD are more likely to experience relationship and marital problems.

In light of all these risk factors, children who struggle with Inattentive ADHD should be provided with support and guidance to help them excel in their academics as well as their social lives. The inability to focus on reading for extended periods of time can be very detrimental to the self-esteem of a child, causing them to become withdrawn and less active. Therefore, special care needs to be taken when dealing with a child who is affected by this disorder.

Inattentive ADHD can be treated using a combination of medication, behavioral therapy, psychotherapy, family counseling, and social skills training. An inattentive ADHD patient can also employ several effective strategies to help them cope with the problem and manage their lives better.

Whether you are suffering from Inattentive ADHD, or you know someone who is affected by the disorder, here are some strategies that may help you manage the problem better. These include:

- ***Set a Time before Beginning an Intensive Task***
Perhaps you have noticed that you tend to get bored easily when reading for extended periods of time. You may want to set a timer before you begin the task so that it serves as a reminder of what you should be doing. This will keep you from getting distracted easily or bored when you are reading

- ***Manage your Environment***
If you have noticed that you tend to get distracted when reading, you can remedy the problem by creating a more conducive environment for reading. Maybe try keeping the curtains closed so that all the activities outside do not interfere with your reading. You may also want to switch off the TV or computer in order to allow yourself to concentrate better

- ***Get More Organized***
Forgetfulness is a common problem for people affected by Inattentive ADHD. It can, however, be solved by simply getting more organized beforehand. Get in the habit of keeping your essential day-to-day items like keys, phone, and wallet in the same place, every time. This will help you minimize the risk of forgetting, hence you will be able to manage your life

better.

- ***Develop a Routine***

Another way in which you can manage ADHD is by developing a routine of the daily tasks you are supposed to carry out. In essence, you should create a schedule outlining all the things you are supposed to do on a daily basis and make an effort to ensure you carry them out.

Hyperactive-Impulsive ADHD

Individuals who are affected with hyperactive ADHD always seem to have a constant need for movement. They may fidget or squirm constantly, or appear to be restless all the time. Due to their constant movement and activity, persons with this type of ADHD may appear to be 'driven by a motor.' Hyperactive-Impulsive ADHD affects both sexes, although children and adult males tend to manifest it more.

Some of the traits of persons with hyperactive-impulsive ADHD include:

- They never seem to be able to sit still
- They tend to fidget and constantly squirm when seated
- They constantly leave their seat in situations where being seated is required, e.g., meetings, classrooms, office
- They often run around or climb on objects inappropriately
- They may talk excessively and tend to interrupt other people when they are speaking
- They often blurt out answers before questions have been completed
- They have a tendency to completing other people's sentences
- They often have difficulty waiting for their turn to speak during conversations
- They may constantly intrude on other people even when not invited or granted permission and disrupt whatever they are doing
- They have difficulty engaging in tasks which require silence
- They tend to act on impulse without thinking about the consequences of their actions
- They often make impulsive comments which are typically not well thought out or inappropriate.
- They tend to touch and play around with objects even when it is not appropriate to the task at hand.

Children and adults with hyperactive-impulsive ADHD tend to be the most disruptive in social situations such as classrooms and workplaces. Due to their seeming lack of foresight when interacting with people, they may come across as rude, narcissistic, and self-absorbed. The impulsive behavior and hyperactivity that characterizes this type of ADHD can take a serious toll on the lives of the affected individuals. It is, therefore, absolutely necessary to manage the disorder effectively.

Treatment for hyperactive-impulsive ADHD typically involves medication, along with behavioral therapy and psychotherapy. The condition can also be effectively managed through several techniques and strategies. These include:

- ***Understanding The Problem and How it Uniquely Manifests in You***
While most people with hyperactive-impulsive ADHD may share some similar symptoms, no two cases are ever completely alike. It is, therefore very essential that you develop an understanding of how the disorder uniquely manifests in your life or in someone else you know. Having a proper grasp on your symptoms and the negative ways in which they affect your life will allow you to implement the right strategies when dealing with the condition

- ***Practice Mindfulness***
Mindfulness can be a great tool for a person's dealing with hyperactive-impulsive ADHD. It allows you to distance yourself from your impulses and urges and gain clarity on the right course of action. When you feel any urge to act impulsively, try to focus on the thoughts and feelings running through you. With regular practice and positive reinforcement, you will become more adept at observing your impulses without letting them control you.

- ***Try Engaging in Activities which Calm and Relax You***
Symptoms of hyperactive-impulsive ADHD tend to become more pronounced when the person is under stress or anxiety. Relaxing may help you calm down when your impulses are triggered by stress factors. You can employ deep-breathing techniques and muscle relaxation exercises to help you calm down until your restlessness and impulsivity dissipate.

Combined-Type ADHD

A combined type is a form of ADHD that is characterized by inattention, hyperactivity, and impulsivity. This subtype of ADHD is by far the most common of all ADHD diagnoses.

ADHD usually manifests in people as predominantly inattentive or predominantly hyperactive-impulsive. When someone manifests symptoms of both subtypes, they will be diagnosed as having combined type ADHD.

There are several factors that may increase a person's risk factor for ADHD. These include:

- ***Genes***

Studies have revealed a correlation between genetics and risk factors for ADHD. Some families have a higher affinity for ADHD due to inherited genes

- ***Environmental Factors during Pregnancy***

Research has shown that environmental factors during pregnancy may increase the risk of ADHD. For instance, an unborn child may develop ADHD after birth if their mother was exposed to toxins during pregnancy.

- ***Brain Injury***

Children who have suffered traumatic blows and injuries to the head are at a very high risk of developing ADHD as they grow.

- ***Drug and Alcohol use During Pregnancy***

Scientific research has revealed that mothers who smoke cigarettes and drink a lot of alcohol while pregnant significantly increases the risk of their child developing ADHD.

While combined ADHD is presently not curable, there are plenty of strategies that can be used to manage the condition effectively. The best strategies usually involve a combination of medication, psychotherapy, and behavioral therapy. However, it is important to realize that not all treatment strategies will work for all cases. You should, therefore, consult with your doctor so that they can evaluate your unique symptoms and recommend the most suitable approach to manage your ADHD.

Poor Functional Vision

Poor vision is another problem that often afflicts children as well as adults, leading to reading problems. Lack of proper functional vision can affect reading in several ways. First, poor vision makes it difficult for one to focus. It can be incredibly difficult for a reader to maintain their focus for extended periods of time when their vision is blurry. Without sustained focus, reading can become incredibly slow and frustrating.

Poor functional vision can also make hand-eye coordination difficult. This is especially more frustrating for people who use a pointer when reading. If you are unable to see while reading, you will find that your speed is significantly slower than it should be. In addition to this, poor vision can severely affect one's self-esteem and confidence. The inability to see properly makes performing tasks such as research and study very harrowing. You may realize that your child no longer completes assignments or school work due to strained vision. This can make them feel inadequate and significantly put a dent in their confidence.

Since vision is very important to reading, it is absolutely essential that you resolve your child's vision problem in order to improve their reading ability. Some of the signs that your child's vision problems may be affecting their reading include:

- They often complain of headaches after reading for short periods of time
- They often close one eye when reading
- Their eyes become sore, red and irritated after reading
- They feel sleepy or fatigued after reading
- They read slowly or skip words

If you have noticed any of these symptoms, you should take immediate action to protect your child's vision from further damage. A visit to an ophthalmologist will help you get the right diagnosis. They will also recommend the right treatment solutions to remedy the vision problem.

Chapter 4: Step 4 – Appreciate the Benefits of Speed Reading

In the previous chapter, we explored the common reading problems that many young learners face when they start learning how to read. We have also discussed the main causes of reading difficulty and how they negatively affect not just the reading comprehension ability of individuals, but also their general lives. We have seen the importance of helping young learners overcome or manage the common reading disorders, and the ways to do so. By managing the common reading difficulties that children and adults face, they can become more fluent at reading comprehension and double their reading speed in a very short amount of time.

However, you may be wondering what exactly is the deal with speed reading, and why people should bother developing fast reading skills. If that is the case, then worry not. In this chapter, we are going to go over some of the advantages that you can enjoy by doubling your reading speed. We will also discuss the numerous benefits that speed reading provides on the brain.

Advantages of Learning How to Read Fast

In the fast-paced world that we live in today, the art of speed reading can be tremendously beneficial to you regardless of your occupation. Whether you are a student or a business professional, you can derive a lot of benefits from doubling your reading speed.

Some of the advantages you can enjoy from learning how to read faster include.

- ***It Will Boost Your Reading Speed***

If you are a voracious reader, you will no doubt agree that learning speed reading can immensely boost average reading speeds. While most people struggle with reading long books, learning the art of speed reading can help you lessen the amount of time you spend reading texts, thereby enabling you to take in more information quicker. This can be very beneficial to your professional life as well as your personal life.

- ***Faster Information Absorption***

Mastering the art of speed reading can greatly enhance the rate at which you absorb information. By doubling your reading speed through the right techniques and practice, you will significantly reduce the amount of time you spend on certain passages and texts. This is because you won't need to reread several times to understand what you are reading. As a result, you will be able to grasp information quickly and easily.

- ***Improved Comprehension Ability***

The art of speed reading goes hand in hand with comprehension ability. After all, there is no point in reading fast if you cannot understand what you are reading. Therefore, practicing speed reading will enhance your reading comprehension abilities and enable you to retain information better.

- ***It Will Make You More Knowledgable***

Developing your reading speed can be highly beneficial to the process of information acquisition. If you are a voracious reader, who likes reading for leisure, learning how to read faster enables you to reduce the amount of time you spend to complete a book. You will, therefore, be able to become more prolific at reading several books on different subjects in a relatively short span of time. This will make you highly knowledgeable in various subjects of interest.

- ***It Improves your Ability to Recall Information Easily***

Learning how to read faster can be very beneficial to your recall ability. By developing your reading speed along with comprehension ability, you will become more skillful at connecting different ideas together when reading. This can greatly improve your ability to remember previous information more easily.

- ***It Empowers You to Cope with Information Overload***

You will no doubt agree that we live in an age where we are flooded with all kinds of information. Without the right coping mechanisms, it is easy for one to become overwhelmed by all this information. However, learning to read fast reduces the amount of time you spend acquiring and interpreting information. You will, therefore, become more empowered to deal with a lot of information by learning and mastering speed reading techniques.

- ***Improves your Time Management Skills***

While reading can be a fun and enjoyable passive hobby, it can also be very time-consuming if your reading speed is average. You may find yourself spending too much time on reading that your other interests or tasks begin to suffer. However, by learning the right speed reading techniques, you can significantly shorten the amount of time reading, thereby allowing yourself time for your other engagements and responsibilities.

- ● *It can Help You Increase Your Opportunities in Life*

Reading is a skill that is essential in many careers. Professionals such as lawyers, researchers, writers, and journalists constantly use their reading abilities in the execution of their tasks. By learning speed reading techniques and doubling your reading speed, you can greatly increase your chances of succeeding in these careers as well as many others. In addition to this, the ability to read fast enables you to become more skillful at connecting pieces of information. This can allow you to come up with novel ideas that you can implement in your personal life, thereby increasing your opportunities.

- ● *It can ease the amount Strain on Your Eyes and Fatigue*

While reading essentially happens passively, being engaged in reading for prolonged durations can cause immense strain on the eyes. It can also lead to fatigue, especially if one uses the wrong body posture when reading. Learning how to read faster significantly reduces the amount of time required to read a given text, thereby minimizing strain on the eyes and fatigue.

Why Speed Reading is Good for the Brain

So far, we have seen the numerous benefits which speed reading offers to individuals who learn the proper speed reading techniques. Learning how to read fast can greatly improve your comprehension, recall ability, and knowledgeability. However, did you know that doubling your reading speed can be good for your brain as well?

Studies have shown that the ability to read faster can tremendously enhance once cognition in a number of areas. One of the ways in which speed reading can improve your cognition is by increasing your focus and attention span. As mentioned before, most people can read at a rate of about 200 words per minute compared to proficient speed readers, who can read at more than double this rate. The reason for this massive difference is that most average-rate readers tend to get distracted when reading. As a result, they end up having to reread sentences or pages to comprehend what they are reading. This usually results in a lot of time getting wasted. Doubling your reading speed, on the other hand, can help you remain focussed and attentive when reading, thereby allowing you to become more skillful at reading comprehension.

Another reason why speed reading is good for the brain is that it enhances memory. Just as we train our muscles to become resilient through fitness and weight exercises, we can train our brains to have better memory through speed reading exercises. These techniques for doubling reading speed train our brains to become more adept at taking in information quickly and retain it more effectively. By mastering speed reading techniques, therefore, you can significantly improve both your working memory as well as your long term memory.

In addition to this, training your brain to read and comprehend information faster and more efficiently enhances your ability to sort out chunks of information and draw out parallels and correlation. This can make you more skillful at reasoning and coming up with accurate deductions on various subjects and topics. Moreover, doubling your reading speed can significantly boost your self-confidence and self-esteem. By learning to read faster and comprehend information quickly, you will open up a world of opportunities to yourself. The skills that you have developed will also make you more empowered to take on the opportunities and improve the overall state of your life and wellbeing.

As you can see, there are plenty of benefits that you can derive from learning how to read faster. By practicing speed reading techniques and doubling your reading speed, you will greatly improve your cognitive faculties and become more adapted to the day-to-day challenges of the fast-paced world today. Developing fast reading skills will also make the act of reading more enjoyable, as you will boost your reading comprehension ability.

Chapter 5: Step 5 – Master the Main Techniques to Improve Speed Reading

So far, we have seen the myriads of advantages which speed reading offers to those bold enough to learn the right fast reading skills. You probably agree now that speed reading can be tremendously beneficial to your career, your personal life, and your interests. In this section, we are going to explore some of the techniques which you can employ to help you enhance your reading speed and comprehension ability.

Contrary to what many people may believe, speed reading is not a skill reserved only for exceptionally intelligent individuals. As a matter of fact, anyone can double their reading speed if they employ the right techniques, have diligent practice and dedication.

Therefore, if you struggle with average reading speeds and are trying to improve your reading comprehension abilities, I assure you it is entirely possible. The seven-speed reading techniques that we are going to discuss in this chapter will help you develop fast reading skills and become highly proficient at reading comprehension. It is my hope that by the end of this chapter, you will be equipped with all the information you need on how to improve your reading speed and abilities.

Scanning

Scanning is one of the best strategies used by students and professionals to help develop their speed reading ability. It essentially involves zapping through your source material to ascertain whether the information contained therein is relevant to your purposes. Scanning is usually employed in academic contexts by students to help them narrow down on specific information or data which they need. It is also very useful in professions that require the analysis of large volumes of information, e.g., law or journalism.

The technique of scanning allows readers to go through a large number of texts and pick out the most important points and main ideas. Scanning can help you to easily pick out the meanings of certain words or find details in extensive passages and excerpts.

Although scanning is a highly beneficial technique for improving speed reading and comprehension, one should refrain from using scanning alone as a reading strategy. Most readers who are overly reliant on scanning typically end up having comprehension problems. This is due to the fact that missing certain pointers or qualifiers can dramatically alter the meaning of a particular text. So, while scanning is a highly useful tool when it comes to reading, research, and study, you should only use it only when necessary.

Here are some of the tips you may want to employ when scanning a source of information for specific facts and details:

- Scan the overall layout of the text you are reading and take note of headers and captions. This will enable you to get a general idea or feel of the themes involved
- Use peripheral vision to capture the main subheaders of the text or passage that you are reading. Employing wide-eyed vision is important when scanning since it allows you to pick up on the general topics of the content you are reading
- Employ a wide-span approach when reading in order to scan the text for details quickly. One way in which you can do this is by reading the page in a zigzag pattern and taking note of any keywords. You can also scan the page vertically, reading from top to bottom then up again.
- Conduct a quick scan of the paragraphs by reading the first word of every sentence. This will help you determine whether the information contained therein is relevant to your research or study.
- Speed up your eye movements when scanning so that you can take in more information faster
- Look out for any special formatting, numbers, images, illustrations, and symbols. These usually serve as pointers in a text and can help you pick up on relevant information more easily.

The technique of scanning can provide plenty of benefits to reading comprehension and general learning. Some of these include:

It Enables you to Grasp Key Ideas in a Text

One of the reasons why scanning is very useful is because it allows you to understand the main ideas in a book, excerpt, or text. By scanning a text thoroughly before reading, you can easily pick up on the main themes and topics in a book. This, in turn, helps you to determine whether the information contained in the text is relevant to your research or study.

It Saves Time

Effectively scanning a text when reading or researching allows you to cut down on the time you spend reading. Through scanning, you can easily narrow down on the important details, thereby eliminating the need to read word-for-word. If used properly, therefore, scanning can make you highly skilled at reading comprehension while also significantly increasing your reading speed.

Makes You More Knowledgable

The art of scanning can also help you expand your knowledge on various subjects and disciplines. The core of any book is usually condensed into chapter boxes, synopsis, and summaries. Therefore, by scanning, you can obtain a lot of information without having to read the entire book.

Scanning is an art that takes a lot of practice to develop. However, the benefits of developing this important reading technique make it worth the effort. With diligence and dedication, you will become good at scanning texts and double your reading speed in no time.

Skimming

Skimming is another useful previewing technique that can help you double your reading speed and improve your comprehension ability. While scanning involves looking over the entire information to pick out particular details, skimming entails reading through the entire text to get an overall impression of the content. Contrary to what many people believe, skimming is not a random process of simply placing your eyes wherever they fall on a given page or text. When it comes to this previewing strategy, what you read is actually more important than what you do not read.

Just as is the case with scanning, skimming is an effective study and research strategy that can help you save a lot of time when reading. However, one should refrain from using only this strategy all the time when reading, as you may end up missing some of the finer details of a piece of information, or misinterpret the text.

Skimming is essentially a strategy that should be employed as a precursor to more thorough and intensive reading. You can, for instance, use skimming to preview the chapters of the textbook before engaging in more detailed reading. This essentially enables you to get a general idea about the contents of the source material. It can also allow you to easily pick up on any differences and similarities compared to other sources.

To become skillful at skimming, it is vital to know what information to look for. Here is a step-by-step guide on how to use skimming to increase your reading speed and comprehension abilities:

1. *Read the Title of the Book*

The first thing you need to do when skimming is to read the title of the book or source material which you are reading. This will provide you with a general idea or main theme of the book, so you can determine whether it is relevant to your research.

2. *Read the Introduction or Preface*

Usually, the introduction of a book provides important clues on the subject matter that is discussed in the chapters. By reading the introduction or preface of the book, you can quickly deduce information contained in the subsequent pages.

3. *Read the First Sentence of Each Paragraph*

The first sentence of a paragraph often provides insight on the topic that is addressed in successive sentences. Therefore, by reading the first sentence, you can easily determine the content of the sentences that follow.

4. *Read Headers and Subheaders*

When skimming, it is absolutely essential to read all the headers and subheaders of your source material. This will give you an overview of the information that is contained in the paragraphs.

5. *Take Note of Illustration, Graphs, and Images*

It is important to take note of any illustrations, graphs, and images that may be present in the book that you are skimming. These serve as pointers, which may help you identify the main details in the information you are reading.

6. Read the Sentences Containing Keywords

When skimming through a given book or text, you should pause momentarily to read sentences that contain keywords. You will likely find important details and facts in these sentences, which will allow you to comprehend the information easily.

7. Read Chapter Summaries If There are Any

Usually, chapter summaries contain a lot of compressed information pertaining to the theme or subject of a book. You can, therefore, gain a general understanding of the main concepts of a book simply by reading through the summary.

You should note that when you skim, you may end up missing a lot of information, which may compromise your understanding of the text. You should, therefore, use this strategy to preview your material before you engage in an in-depth study. With daily practice, you will eventually become very skillful at skimming, thus increasing your reading speed dramatically.

Skipping

Skipping words is a problem which many children and adults face when reading. However, skipping can also be employed as a strategy to enhance one's speed reading abilities. When used in this manner, the reader skips the sections of a given text which contain irrelevant, unnecessary, or redundant information.

Skipping is a strategy that requires a lot of tact and discernment. This is because when you skip sections of a given text or book which contains crucial info, it may result in comprehension problems. A skilled reader essentially knows when it is appropriate to skip a given section of a book or source material. Unskilled readers, on the other hand, may skip entire sections simply because they feel bored or uninterested. This is a trait otherwise known as selective reading.

Being selective when reading is not proper practice, as it can severely hinder comprehension. Due to this, you should only employ skipping as a speed reading technique only when it is necessary.

Some of the instances where it may be appropriate to skip sections of a given
text include:

- If a section does not contain any new information
- If a given section does not contain information that is relevant to your
  purposes

Skipping is a very useful strategy to increase your reading speed, especially if
you tend to read a lot of material. It can help you save a lot of time when
reading, without compromising your understanding of the material. Skipping
also works best when reading particular subjects from media sources. For
instance, when reading a newspaper or magazine, you may be interested in a
specific section, say sports or fashion. In such a case, it would be more
practical to skip the sections you are not interested in and go directly to the
ones that pick your interest.

Minimized Subvocalization

If you are like most people, you can probably hear yourself in your head
when reading. That's because when we are learning to read as kids, we are
taught to say the words silently in our heads while we read. This is a
phenomenon known as subvocalization.
While the habit of subvocalization may seem very natural to us, it is, in fact,
a bad reading habit, as it can seriously impair our ability to read fast.

Subvocalization usually makes people read at a much slower rate, and can
greatly put a strain on any efforts to improve reading speed. Essentially,
subvocalization makes one only able to read as fast as they speak. So, in
order to increase their reading speed, one has to overcome this habit or
minimize it at the very least. However, changing the habit of subvocalization
is not as easy as it may seem. In most cases, it may not be possible to
eliminate subvocalization in your reading practice entirely. In light of this, it
may be more practical to work on reducing it instead.

If you have a habit of subvocalizing when reading, here are some of the tips
that you can apply to help you reduce them in order to increase your reading
speed:

- ***Use Your Finger to Guide Your Eyes When Reading***

One of the most effective strategies to deal with subvocalization is using the finger as a guide on the text when reading. You should try running your finger along with the page of the texts you are reading. This helps distract your mind from the voice in your head, thereby helping minimize subvocalization. As a result, you will find that your reading speed has significantly increased.

• *Devise Techniques to Distract Your Mind*

You can also minimize subvocalization by coming up with simple but effective ways to distract your mind as you read. For instance, you can chew gum or lick a candy stick while you read. This will keep your mind preoccupied, thereby reducing the impulse to vocalize words in your head when reading.

• *Listen to Music as You Read*

Listening to music while reading can be a highly effective strategy to deal with subvocalization. This is because it keeps your mind distracted, and reduces the urge to sound words in your head while reading. Listening to music can also greatly enhance your concentration when reading. However, the choice of music is an important factor to consider. Calm and relaxing instrumental music usually works best when reading. On the other hand, music with lyrics or upbeat genres of music should be avoided when reading since it can be very disruptive to the whole exercise.

• *Try Reading Faster than You Normally Do*

If you constantly sound words in your head when reading, you may want to try reading faster than usual to remedy the problem of subvocalization — attempting to read faster than your normal speed can help you reduce the number of words you say in your head, thereby reducing subvocalization when reading. It is also good practice for speed reading since it helps you become more attentive and focused when reading. Eventually,with a lot of practice and consistency, you will get better at reading faster without subvocalizing too much.

While the habit of subvocalization may be detrimental to fast reading, it can also be advantageous sometimes. For instance, subvocalizing unfamiliar words that you encounter when reading can help you expand your vocabulary, improve your pronunciation, and exercise your memory. All these are highly beneficial to developing speed reading skills.

So, when it comes to subvocalization, less is always more. As you reduce your impulse to sound words in your head when reading, you will discover that your reading speed has increased dramatically.

Chunking

Chunking is one of the main speed reading techniques which students and professionals use to enhance their reading comprehension ability. Essentially, chunking entails breaking up long strings of information into smaller groups or 'chunks' such that the resulting groups are easier to comprehend and commit to memory.

Studies have shown that chunking can greatly enhance the reading comprehension abilities of poor readers. This speed reading technique can also significantly improve the working memory of readers, both young and old. This strategy is highly useful as a speed reading technique since it reduces the cognitive load on readers, thereby making them better at processing information.

Chunking is a strategy that is typically employed to help children and poor readers develop their speed reading abilities. If you are thinking of using chunking as a tool to help your child improve their reading comprehension, here is a guide on how you may go about it:

- Select a passage or text that is appropriate for their age
- Break up the text into shorter separate sections
- Let your child read each section individually and assess their comprehension. You can ask them questions to determine whether they have understood what they have read
- Have your child jot down short summaries for each section they have read.This will help them remember the information a lot easier
- Once they have practiced enough, encourage them to use this strategy by themselves

The practice of chunking can be very beneficial to reading comprehension in several ways. First, chunking improves one's recall ability. Breaking up long texts into simpler and more manageable groups makes it possible for one to remember the main concepts as well as details in a given text. The chunking strategy also involves the use of other reading strategies, such as scanning and skimming. This allows one to develop speed reading skills in a more holistic and comprehensive manner.

Chunking can also significantly improve one's peripheral vision. The practice of focussing on word groups as opposed to single words trains the eye to be able to pick out minute details, which may not be precisely in focus.

Finger Tracking

The use of a finger to track the text when reading is a practice which many children are taught when they first learn how to read. Once they are past elementary schooling, learners are usually expected to be able to read using their eyes only, without the aid of a finger or pointer. However, there are many instances in which finger tracking might be beneficial even for advanced students. Struggling readers and those with learning disabilities such as dyslexia and ADHD can experience a lot of difficulties trying to read without the help of a pointer. For this reason, finger tracking is a highly effective strategy that should be encouraged in order to help poor readers, develop fast reading skills, and improve their comprehension abilities.

One of the main benefits of using a pointer or finger to track while reading is that it helps young readers develop proper directional tracking. While most adults are used to the idea of reading texts from left to write, beginner students often struggle with this. It is important to note that the left-to-right tracking that is commonly used in written English literature is more arbitrary than natural. Therefore, it would be wrong to expect a young child to naturally read left to write without any form of training or practice. The use of a pointer when reading, however, helps the child become acclimated to left-to-right directional tracking, and eventually, it becomes effortless.

Another reason why finger-pointing or pacing is beneficial when reading is that it allows one to focus on a specific line of text without being distracted by the ones below or above it. This can greatly increase reading speed and enhance comprehension. In addition to this, pacing with the finger while reading increases concentration, thereby allowing one to read much faster and retain information better. Also, using the finger to track your reading keeps more parts of your body engaged in the reading process. This can help minimize distractions when reading, thereby improving your reading comprehension. Moreover, finger tracking can aid readers in correcting any improper techniques they may have developed early on when they started learning how to read.

In light of these benefits that finger tracking provides to reading comprehension, it is vital that young learners, as well as older students, are encouraged to adopt this technique. When combined with other speed reading techniques such as scanning and skimming, finger tracking can drastically increase one's reading speed in a very short amount of time.

Faster Page Turning

The amount of time a reader spends turning a page when reading might seem like a trivial matter. However, studies have shown that page-turning speed has a significant influence on the reading speed of an individual. Most average readers spend about 5 seconds turning the pages of a book while reading, which is about the same amount of time it takes many skilled speed readers to read an entire page.

Slow page-turning can be very detrimental to one's reading speed. If you spend 5 seconds to turn a page, you end up wasting several minutes when reading any text. Slow page-turning can also negatively affect one's comprehension. This is because it makes you lose track of the flow of ideas that the writer is trying to convey.

In order to increase your reading speed and enhance your comprehension abilities, you need to overcome the problem of slow page-turning and become more skilled at turning the pages faster. One of the techniques which you can employ to increase your page-turning speed is 'breaking' the books back. In order to do so, you need to hold the book with both hands and bend it backward such that the covers are touching each other. Practice binding the book every 20 to 25 pages so that the pages lie flat. This eliminates the need to keep holding down the pages, which often leads to slower reading. Obviously, you should only bend the books that you own, not ones that you have borrowed from a friend or the library. Also, page-turning is more appropriate when working with paperback books since hardcover books naturally lie flat on their own.

By practicing the skill of bending books while reading, you will significantly reduce the amount of time you spend turning pages as you read.

Consequently, your reading speed and comprehension abilities will significantly improve.

Chapter 6: Step 6 – Improve Your Reading Comprehension

The ability to read and comprehend a text is a highly complex cognitive process that requires the coordination of several different brain functions. It usually also demands that we work through different layers of context and meaning in order to accurately interpret a given text and grasp the ideas that are being conveyed. Due to these complexities, reading comprehension is a problem which many people struggle with even as adults. If left unresolved, poor reading comprehension abilities may lead to literacy problems in both children and adults.

There are plenty of factors that affect one's reading and comprehension abilities. These include poorly developed education systems, high poverty, and unemployment rates, and lack of interest in reading. Nevertheless, speed reading and good comprehension are skills that anyone can develop with proper practice and dedication.

If you are trying to improve your reading comprehension abilities, here are some of the tips that might find useful.

Expand Your Vocabulary

One of the most effective ways to improve your reading comprehension is by building your vocabulary. Your ability to read and comprehend texts is heavily reliant on your understanding of the meaning of words and how they are used in different contexts. As far as proper comprehension is concerned, it is much better to be able to understand the context in which certain words are used instead of trying to memorize the meaning of words from the dictionary. In all likelihood, you will probably never use most of the words that you memorize by reading through a dictionary. It is, therefore, far more beneficial to understand how the words are practically used in written contexts as well as in conversations.

However, improving your vocabulary is not as simple to do as it sounds. You will need to spend a lot of time reading, notating, and trying to decipher the meaning of words through analysis of context. Nevertheless, by improving your vocabulary, you will greatly enhance your reading speed as well as your comprehension abilities.

Here are some of the tips and techniques which you can employ to build your vocabulary.

1. *Get into the Habit of Reading A lot*

In order to rapidly improve your vocabulary, the first thing you need to do is develop the habit of reading a lot. Instead of spending copious amounts of time watching movies or chatting with friends, grab a good novel or literary work, and fully engage yourself in it for a couple of hours. The more books you read, the more words you will encounter, and you will learn how the words are used in context. This will greatly benefit your reading and comprehension abilities as you will be able to understand the information you are reading quickly.

2. *Use a Dictionary*

Having a dictionary close to you while you read can greatly enhance your vocabulary and make you a faster and more efficient reader. As you read, you will encounter unfamiliar words that you can easily look up in the dictionary in order to grasp their meaning and usage. You can also use a thesaurus to look up synonyms and antonyms of the words you come across during your reading sessions. This will help you further expand your vocabulary and become a more proficient reader.

3. *Keep Notes*

One of the best practices that will help you improve your vocabulary and become a more skillful reader is keeping notes. When reading, try to keep a list of any new words that you come across. This will make it much easier for you to refer back to the words and gradually assimilate them into your vocabulary. The practice of keeping notes will also boost your morale to learn more words as you look back on all the words you have learned. This will eventually make your vocabulary richer and empower you to become a better reader.

4. *Practice*

When it comes to improving your vocabulary, the saying that 'Practice makes perfect' rings very true. Using the new words you have learned in your conversations with people and in writing can significantly improve your comprehension. The more fluent you become in using the new words that you learn, the more proficient you will become as a reader.

Manage Your Environment to Eliminate Distractions

You are probably well aware of just how difficult it can be to read in a noisy environment. Reading in an unconducive environment can be very distracting for you, especially if you already struggle with reading problems. Distractions can greatly slow down your reading pace and negatively affect your comprehension.

In light of this, it is absolutely essential that you create a conducive environment before you pick up a book to start reading. Ensure that the TV and any other electronic gadgets are turned off before you settle down to read. If you have a smartphone, you should put it on silent or airplane mode to minimize the chances of getting distracted by phone calls, notifications, and text messages. In case it is not possible to remove all distractions from your reading environment, you may want to move to a more congenial and less distracting environment, for instance, the library or study room.

In some cases, the distractions may be internally based rather than external. For instance, you may find yourself getting distracted by intrusive thoughts and worries. In such a case, you may want to employ some relaxation techniques to ease your mind in order to focus better. Breathing exercises can help reduce stressors, which may be distracting to you while you read. You can also play some relaxing music at lower volumes to help your mind relax and improve your focus when reading.

By taking the necessary steps to manage your external as well as the internal environment, you will improve your concentration when reading so that you can read faster and comprehend better.

Practice Reading for Pleasure

In order to improve your reading comprehension, you need to practice consistently. And the only way to do so is by reading a lot. However, reading can be a very mentally and physically draining exercise, especially if it is done out of obligation. I'm sure reading a 200-page work-related report is not anyone's idea of fun. So how best should you practice your reading skills? Simple. Make reading a fun exercise that you enjoy doing instead of a chore, which you hate but have to do anyway.

If you are trying to improve your reading comprehension but do not enjoy reading very much, here are some of the tips which might make reading a more pleasurable exercise for you.

i) Read Books about Topics You Find Interesting

One of the ways in which you can make reading a more pleasurable activity for you is to choose books about subjects that interest you. Instead of trying to force your way through a book on a topic you find boring, why not select one that matches your passions? By selecting a book on a topic that you like for your reading practice, you will be more motivated and enthusiastic about reading.

ii) Use Audiobooks to Aid Your Reading

Another great strategy you can employ to make your reading more enjoyable is to read along to audiobooks. Listening to audiobooks related to the books you are reading provides a much more interactive experience, which can increase your enthusiasm for reading, thereby allowing you to develop your reading skills.

iii) Create Your Own Special Reading Space

If you struggle with reading, you can make reading a lot more enjoyable by creating a conducive reading area for yourself. Select a location or room which you like and prop it up to make it more congenial for reading. If you are averse to bright lights, you may want to consider fitting low-light bulbs in your reading space to make it more comfortable and conducive for your reading sessions. This will make reading a more pleasurable activity for you and thus act as a motivating factor to make you read more.

Discuss What You Are Reading with a Friend

There are some instances when discussing the text you are reading with a friend can greatly enhance your comprehension. If you find yourself struggling to comprehend the text you are reading, it might be beneficial for you to discuss it with a friend who has not read it. Articulating your thoughts on the book to a friend can aid you in picking out the areas where your comprehension is limited. You might even realize that your understanding is very spot on once you try explaining your thoughts to someone who has never read the text you are reading.

Even if there is no one close by to discuss your opinions with, you can still use this strategy very effectively. If you have a pet, you can take momentary breaks in-between reading sessions to explain your understanding of your text to it. Obviously, the pet has no way of understanding what you are saying, and so it won't be an actual discussion. However, by practicing this approach, you will be able to determine your comprehension rate and equip yourself with the knowhow on how to navigate any problems you may have. So, the next time you are reading through a text, take the time to implement this strategy. In doing so, you will greatly enhance your comprehension abilities and become a more proficient and skillful reader.

Pause When You Lose Focus and Reflect on What You Have Read

Another great strategy to employ when developing your reading comprehension is a reflection. When you get confused as you are reading, take a momentary break to think about what you have read and how much you have understood. If possible, make a mental summary of all the important information that you have grasped from the text you are reading. Once you have determined your comprehension rate, you can proceed reading with the summation of key points and details in mind. Doing this will allow you to keep track of your reading and therefore boost your reading comprehension. It will also enable you to retain the information better.

Chapter 7: Step 7 – Reevaluate Your Current Reading Strategies

In order to improve your reading speed and reading comprehension abilities, it is absolutely essential that you first analyze the strategies you are currently using and their effectiveness. This will help you determine the success rate of your reading style as well as the limitations that your strategy suffers from.

You can begin to evaluate your existing reading strategies by studying the way you read. Start by selecting unfamiliar reading material, for instance, a novel, essay or textbook. Read your selected test material as you would normally do and pay close attention to your comprehension rate, attention span, and energy levels. This will provide you with useful pointers on areas where you may be lagging behind.

If you have noticed that your comprehension rate is lower or your attention tends to dwindle, you can practice reading slower at first and progressively build up your speed. For instance, if you realize that you tend to lose focus after 30 minutes of reading, take note of this fact and try to increase this time gradually. Try not to force yourself to read for prolonged periods of time at once since this can lead to fatigue and irritability, which may lower your reading speed as well as your comprehension. Instead, begin by reading for your maximum focus time, say 30 minutes, then take a short break to absorb the information and refresh. You can, thereafter, resume your reading and try to surpass your previous record. Eventually, you will realize that your reading speed is gradually increasing without compromising your comprehension. Try not to get frustrated if your focus time is really short at first. With time and practice, you will be able to double your reading speed and become more skillful at reading comprehension.

You may also realize that your reading speed and reading comprehension problem stems from the source material rather than reading the time. Perhaps you experience difficulty with comprehending the themes, ideas, and details in a given text. If this is the case, you may want to consider selecting a book that is on par with your level of comprehension. It might be difficult, for instance, to read and comprehend a book on legislation if you have no background in legal matters. In such a scenario, it would be more beneficial to switch to a book on a subject you are familiar with. When it comes to developing your reading speed, the complexity of the subject is not as important as the fact that you can comprehend what you are reading. Therefore, endeavor to begin with simpler books that you can understand more easily. Over time and with diligent practice, you will find that your reading speed and reading comprehension abilities have drastically improved.